SIVANANDA : DAY-TO-DAY

PLATINUM JUBILEE SERIES: JANUARY 13th, 2011

SIVANANDA
DAY-TO-DAY

By

SRI SWAMI SANTANANDA

Published by

THE DIVINE LIFE SOCIETY

P.O. SHIVANANDANAGAR—249 192

Distt. Tehri-Garhwal, Uttarakhand, Himalayas, India

www.sivanandaonline.org

Price]   **2011**   [Rs. 85/-

First Edition: 1960
Second Edition: 2007
Third Edition: 2011

[500 Copies]

ISBN 81-7052-200-5

EO 3

Published by Swami Padmanabhananda for
The Divine Life Society, Shivanandanagar, and printed by him
at the Yoga-Vedanta Forest Academy Press,
P.O. Shivanandanagar—249 192, Distt. Tehri-Garhwal,
Uttarakhand, Himalayas, India
www.sivanandaonline.org

SRI SWAMI SIVANANDA

Born on the 8th September, 1887, in the illustrious family of Sage Appayya Dikshitar and several other renowned saints and savants, Sri Swami Sivananda had a natural flair for a life devoted to the study and practice of Vedanta. Added to this was an inborn eagerness to serve all and an innate feeling of unity with all mankind.

His passion for service drew him to the medical career; and soon he gravitated to where he thought that his service was most needed. Malaya claimed him. He had earlier been editing a health journal and wrote extensively on health problems. He discovered that people needed right knowledge most of all; dissemination of that knowledge he espoused as his own mission.

It was divine dispensation and the blessing of God upon mankind that the doctor of body and mind renounced his career and took to a life of renunciation to qualify for ministering to the soul of man. He settled down at Rishikesh in 1924, practised intense austerities and shone as a great Yogi, saint, sage and Jivanmukta.

In 1932 Swami Sivananda started the Sivanandashram. In 1936 was born The Divine Life Society. In 1948 the Yoga-Vedanta Forest Academy was organised. Dissemination of spiritual knowledge and training of people in Yoga and Vedanta were their aim and object. In 1950 Swamiji undertook a lightning tour of India and Ceylon. In 1953 Swamiji convened a 'World Parliament of Religions'. Swamiji is the author of over 300 volumes and has disciples all over the world, belonging to all nationalities, religions and creeds. To read Swamiji's works is to drink at the Fountain of Wisdom Supreme. On 14th July, 1963 Swamiji entered Mahasamadhi.

PUBLISHERS' NOTE

It is admitted that Saint Sivananda is the channel for the Lord's Grace to flow into the heart of man. By his sight or Sankalpa, he can confer blessings—material and spiritual—on the devotee. He has toured all over the land and delivered numerous lectures. He has written over three hundred books which guide the lives of people all over the world.

But that is not all. Sri Swamiji excels all other saints, in the human element that is predominent in him. He loves to mix with all; and to show how every man in his everyday life leads the life divine. He shows us how our prosaic actions can be sublimated into Yoga.

All this he does by his own example. To spiritual aspirants, therefore, his thoughts, words and deeds are of the greatest import.

A close and devout disciple of Sri Gurudev and an earnest spiritual aspirant, Sri Swami Santananda has, in this volume, brought together the wonderful lessons that all can learn from the daily actions of Sri Gurudev. He has gathered the pearls of wisdom, inspired words of Truth, as they fell from his lips, and presented them in a charming way, that would inspire all.

—**The Divine Life Society**

SIVANANDA LITERATURE –
A MODERN EXPRESSION TO ANCIENT
SCRIPTURES

IN THE IMAGE OF THE MASTER

If Sivananda's Literature is the echo of the ancient Upanishads, Sivananda himself stands as an expression of that age-old literature. Sivananda Literature proves to us what Sivananda himself is because a beautiful, soul-stirring literature springs, not from any superficial intellectual knowledge, but always from the depths and fullness of a heart which spontaneously expresses the inner realisation of the spirit within. Sivananda Literature is thus the mirror which reflects Sivananda himself.

If today Sivananda Literature has awakened the inner spirit of mankind far and wide, all over the globe, it is not because of a mere intellectual out burst, spilling out, without any originality, the collective gathering of empirical dogmas and theories from various sources, but exclusively because it is the very expression of his inner experience, of his inner personality. So to say, he has expressed himself in his literature as he himself is, in reality.

DISTINGUISHING MARKS OF SIVANANDA LITERATURE

Sivananda Literature has induced in man the taste to evolve, to grow and expand in the life material and in the life spiritual as well. It has induced in man the desire to develop the right understanding towards life and its purpose, its way and the goal. Lastly, it has induced in man an eagerness to mould himself from the human into the Divine.

Sivananda Literature is meant not merely for the educated

vii

classes. It is like an open-air theatre, widely open to all, young and old, male and female, literate and illiterate, without the least distinction of caste, colour, creed or race.

For the young man just stepping into the field of life, not having enough strength to face its adverse conditions, Sivananda Literature is a blood tonic which nourishes his entire personality, prepares him and makes him march forward boldly to face the hard game.

To the middle-aged house-holder who is in a fix, not able to face the tribulations of family ties, perplexed as to how to walk the way in the long run of life, Sivananda Literature is a Guiding Light which illumines the royal road and takes him safely till the end of his journey.

Swamiji's method of disseminating the ancient gospel in a most appealing manner, applicable to the modern man, is something unique of its kind.

The most beautiful aspect of it is that you need not go in search of his literature which comes to your very door to greet you, to guide you, to serve you, to comfort and console you in a miraculous way with breathless earnestness and boundless love.

Swami Sivananda serves through his literature—not the body, but the soul. Sivananda Literature is food for the soul. Swamiji sits in a remote corner of Bharatavarsha on the sacred banks of the Ganges. The Ganges flows only in India and that also in a limited area. But, Sivananda Literature, the inexhaustible wisdom of Swamiji flows in the hearts of millions enabling them to reap the rich harvest of ever-lasting peace and immortality.

INDISCRIMINATE CHARITY OF
SPIRITUAL KNOWLEDGE

Swami Sivananda's methods of spreading spiritual knowledge among humanity at large may, sometimes, even look queer, but they are cent per cent fruitful. The moment Swamiji comes across an address, immediately he will send a parcel of his books to the person concerned. Swamiji is not particular even to know whether the person to whom the books are sent is spiritual-minded and is interested in spiritual books.

For the onlooker, this may appear to be a wasteful method, but Swamiji would say, in his calm and cool way: "Don't worry, if the person does not like it, it will be useful to someone somewhere."

Yes, it is quite true. Swamiji's writings which are not mere words of poetic imagination, but sober truths of a perennial philosophy, the immortal voice of the ancient saints and seers, always reach the hands of aspirants longing after liberation, wherever they may be.

Swami Sivananda is not bothered when a person writes abruptly: "Sir, I have no interest in these spiritual books. I don't need them any more." The efforts of Swamiji to spread the Gospel of Divine Life, the only mission of his own life, have no selfish motive behind them. Therefore it is that his efforts have not gone in vain. They have brought forth wonderful fruits. Thousands of aspirants all over the world are daily awakened by Sivananda Literature.

LIFE-TRANSFORMING POWER OF SIVANANDA
LITERATURE—INSTANCES REAL LIFE

It is Swami Sivananda's "Spiritual Lessons" casually found in a second-hand bookshop which transformed the life of Dr. Chellamma, an eye-surgeon of Madras, who was engrossed

ix

in the usual pursuit of worldly life and family attachment, induced her to renounce the world and make her blossom forth into Swami Sivananda-Hridayananda, who now utilises her profession as a worship unto the Lord through her selfless service to the hundreds of poor eye-patients in the Sivananda Eye Hospital.

It is an article of Swamiji found in "My Magazine", by chance, that inspired and elevated Sridhar, a boy belonging to a rich family of luxurious life, made him embrace Sannyasa and turned him into Swami Chidananda, now a shining glory to The Divine Life Society.

It is a single sentence in "Students' Success" which awakened the inner spirit of Shri V.L. Nagaraj of the Postal Department in Banglore when he opened, out of curiosity, a book addressed to somebody else, from a parcel which got untied during transit. The transformation which took place in that single soul has, in its turn, brought about the transformation of hundreds of lives in Bangalore. As a result of it all, a wonderful and dynamic Divine Life Centre flourishes in Bangalore today, having a press of its own and disseminating the gospel of Divine Life through the free distribution of books and pamphlets.

Instances are brought to light every day of how, in a miraculous and astounding manner, aspirants get Swamiji's literature and get themselves transformed. Sivananda Literature is a powerful magnet. When, for the sake of curiosity, you glance at it, you are caught up. You cannot help finishing the book to the end. You cannot help being inspired and elevated. You cannot help getting your materialistic outlook entirely changed. Such is the glory, such is the grandeur and such is the splendour of Sivananda Literature. Every word of this Divine Literature has life in it. Those words go straight into your heart, tear to pieces all your atheistic conclusions and awaken the spirit which is lying dormant behind them all.

However much the squirrel may try, by sponging its tail, will it be ever possible for it to empty the ocean?

Such is my attempt to write about Sivananda-Literature, the Ocean of Wisdom.

CONTENTS

xiii

xiv

xv

SIVANANDA: DAY-TO-DAY

13th MARCH 1959

SAGE OF BOUNDLESS COMPASSION

The Ganges was shining like a silvery carpet in the bright morning sun, and the reflection of the Himalayas in it was like a beautiful design patterned on the carpet.

It was 9-30 a.m. A group of devotees from Malaya and some other visitors were waiting eagerly in front of Swamiii's Kutir. The call came. Doors were opened. All rushed in to have Darshan of Swamiji, the LIGHT HOUSE, that guides the humanity to the shore of immortality.

In the midst of the crowd there was an old poor, diseased person. Somehow he came to the front and sat before Swamiji. After explaining his difficulties he demanded twenty rupees from Swamiji. Swamiji in His boundless compassion took pity on him but gave only Rs. 12/-. Again the old man pleaded for twenty. Swamiji flatly refused and asked Sri Satyagnanam to give him a tin of milk powder and coffee. We were surprised to see this unusual attitude of Swamiji. We were wondering why Swamiji, the generous hearted, refused him the amount he demanded. Immediately Swamiji himself turned to our side, with a saintly smile cleared our doubt.

"He has cultivated the bad habit of drinking. If I give him more money, he will drink more and spoil his health."

We human beings with our physical eyes see only the outward personality but Swamiji, the sage with His X-ray eyes sees the inner heart and acts accordingly.

CONTRADICTORY EXPERIENCES

Atmaramji: Swamiji, if some drink coffee at night they get sound sleep, but it is just the opposite in my case.

Swamiji: That is the beauty. Castor Oil for some relieve

19

constipation and for some increase it, what do you say for this? That which is nectar for one becomes poison for another. This is the mystery, This clearly shows that there is no truth in the object. As you are, so you see and experience. The truth about the object lies only in the truth about the subject. Therefore know Thyself and be free.

THE WORLD GUIDE

The Malaya devotees came one by one and prostrated before Swamiji. One should clearly see the supreme satisfaction and joy on their face when they prostrated before the Sage.

Swamiji proceeded towards the office. Amongst the devotees and disciples who were following Swamiji, one could spot out an American, an African, a German, an English man, an Australian, all mixing with each other as if they belong to a single loving family. The whole procession gave us an idea that Swamiji, the WORLD GUIDE (Jagat Guru) was leading the whole world towards the ultimate goal.

After the Kirtan and prayer Swamiji started his routine work. Swamiji's table was filled with sweets and fruits brought by the Malaya devotees. They were distributed immediately.

THE KAMADHENU

Santosh, a disciple of Swamiji entered the office and prostrated.

Santosh: Swamiji, I have written a beautiful article. I will bring it soon.

Swamiji: Very Glad. What shall I give you now?

Santosh: Swamiji, I want four Iddlys....

Swamiji: Only four iddlys......I will give you eight daily.

Santosh: No Swamiji, whenever I bring articles you can give me four iddlys. But I want them from your Kitchen

Swamiji: Phoo . . . That is all agreed.

Santosh left the office with a contented smile.

Swamiji's heart is like an open treasure-chest. Anybody can go and get anything, they like. Whatever you aspire for, that alone will be given to you. If you want Iddlys you will get. If you want material comforts you will get it. If you aspire for knowledge and wisdom you will get that also. The choice is left to you. According to your aspiration God showers His Grace.

BURY THE PAST

Pointing towards the packet of fruits lying on the table Swamjiji enquired for whom it was kept. "It is kept for Rigo, Swamiji," replied Sri S.

*Swamiji:-*Don't call her Rigo. Her name is Lalitananda.

Miss Rigo the American disciple was initated into Sannyas on Sivaratri day, and is now known as Lailithananda. By His remark Swamiji reminded all of us that a Sannyasi shoud forget all about his Poorvashrama life. He must die to his lower self and learn to live in the spirit.

REINCARNATION

Just then, Sri M.K. Pandit, an old gentleman, native of Udaipur, settled in America came near and prostrated.

M.K. Pandit: Swamiji Maharaj I have heard about your greatness, your wonderful teachings, your wonderful Mission. Today I had your Darshan and I am blessed. Swamiji, is it possible for a soul with a male body to take a female body in the next incarnation?

Swamiji: O Yes. The soul must undergo various experiences in different bodies. In the male body the soul experiences the qualities of boldness, strength, etc., and patience, mercy, kindness, forgiveness, etc., in the female body. Moreover neither a man is a full man nor a woman, a full woman. There is

woman in man, and man in woman also. There are animal traits
also in man. There is dog in some men, there is donkey in some,
there is jackal in some and tiger in other. Whichever quality is
predominant the soul takes that particular body with that quality, in the next incarnation. Therefore develop divine qualities.
You will evolve quickly and become divinity itself in the end.

M.K. Pandit: Thank you Swamiji, very much. My doubt is
cleared now. When I go back I will try to disseminate your
teachings.

WHO IS SIVANANDA?

After Maha Mrityunjaya Mantra and Santi Path,
Swamiji took photograph with the Malayan devotees and was
coming back to his Kutir. On the way he noticed Swami C.
standing in the hot sun without shoes or umbrella.

Swamiji: O Ji Don't come without shoes in this hot sun. It
is not good for your health.

This is how Swamiji takes care of his disciples. By these
actions he clearly proves that he is not only the Guru, but one's
father and mother and, friend and relative, nay everything else.

Swamiji was entering his Kutir. A person approached him
and asked at what time he can have private talk with Swamiji.

Just a word slipped from Swamiji, after a pause.

"ETERNITY"

Only on very very rare occasions Siva shows us his real
Swaroopa, what he is in reality. Sivananda in reality is not the
Sivananda as we see. He is not merely this 6 feet figure. He is
the All-pervading Consciousness, the SIVA HIMSELF, and THAT
which stands unchanged for ETERNITY. What when, how and
where can you talk to Him. He is the very LIGHT which makes
you to talk and think. THAT LIGHT which is within you is
SIVANANDA, in reality.

14th MARCH 1959

LESSON IN FRIENDSHIP

After the night Satsang, Swamiji introduced Sr R., a devotee from Malaya to Sri S.H. Few words, they saluted each other and kept quiet. Noticing this Swamiji remarked:

Swamiji: Oji as soon as you meet a new person you must talk to him or her voluntarily and nicely. You must make the person feel homely within short time. You should not keep any reserved attitude. This is the secret of developing good friendship with one and all.

THE FIELD FOR TALENTS

Today morning Dr. Miss Kripalani from Delhi had Swamiji's Darshan in his Kutir. Sri Atmaram ji introduced her to Swamiji.

Swamiji: Oh You are a doctor! You look like a college student, not as a M.B.B.S. doctor. Acchaji kindly come and stay here during your holiday and do some selfless service in our hospital. It will purify your heart. Can you?

Miss Kripalani: Yes Swamiji, but is there a maternity hospital here, Swamiji, I have specialised in Maternity.

Swamiji: Don't worry. We will open a new maternity hospital for you.

Sri Kripalani stood wonderstruck. She never even imagined that Swamiji will open a maternity hospital for her sake.

Swamiji's compassion in the evolution of all human beings is such, he will make use of anybody with any kind of talent. He somehow provides them an opportunity, induces and inspires them to do some selfless service in some way according to their taste and talent, and makes them evolve, grow and expand.

THE ADHYATMIC ARMY

While in the office Sri Ramanathan Chettiar was giving the reports of the activities in Malaya D.L.S. Swamiji gave him the following advices.

Swamiji: In every area you must form a band of workers. They should be the Adhyatmic soldiers with the spirit of selfless service and dedication. They should have the knowledge of first aid and home science. They should go to the people and serve some hours daily. They can even go to some hospitals and offer their services to the poor patients. This band of selfless workers should be given the name D.L.S. Army. By these methods you can keep the continuous flow of the Divine Life Movement in Kualalumpur.

15th MARCH 1959

NAME AND NATURE

Swamji gave Darshan this morning by 10 a.m. He was in a very jovial mood. The way in which he greets everyone with appropriate remarks to the person concerned is something marvellous and by that he makes each one think that Swamiji belongs to him only.

A devotee from Kualalumpur came and prostrated.

Swamiji: What is the name of your daughter?

Devotee: My daughter's name is Satgunam (means Good Charactered).

Swamiji: Sat Gunam? Has she quarrelsome nature. Is she good to you? Or she is Satgunam only in her name?

Devotee: No Swamiji, She is very good to me. She respects, adores and serves me also nicely.

Swamiji: That is it. One should prove worthy of his name. Some people use to keep very nice names but their character is just the opposite. What is the use of having the name of "Annapoorna" but not giving a morsel of food to any poor man. Miss Rosy may be like Rose only externally but with full of thorns inside. Mr. Broadman will be broad only in his body and will be narrow-minded in heart. As is the name so should be the character.

All enjoyed the instructive joke and burst into laughter. Swamiji's humour is not merely humour, but humour coated wisdom, which brings home to you the truths in an easy manner.

EQUAL VISION

After the office work Swamiji took photographs with a military officer and a press reporter from Delhi. He was coming back to his Kutir. Four or five beggars were standing on the way. Suddenly to the surprise of us all, Swamiji called those poor beggars to his side and asked Sri Purushottam to take snaps. Then he gave each one rupee and sent them away. Both the press reporter and the military officer were dumbfounded to see Swamiji's simplicity and equal vision among the rich and poor.

WITNESS-CONSCIOUSNESS

There was a grand Pada Pooja today conducted by the Malayan devotees. After the Pada Puja photos were taken. Each family in that group took separate photograph with Swamiji. With every snapshot the group were changing one by one but Swamiji himself was there sitting unchanged.

It appeared as if Swamiji was the Unchanging Absolute, witnessing the changing phenomena which come and go.

THE VISION OF WISDOM

Swamiji was coming to the Night Satsang. Sri Swami Paripoornananda, came and bowed to Swamiji.

Swamiji: Paripoornam Maharaj! have you sent those books to the Sivananda Cultural Association, Delhi? Have you written them a letter?

Paripoornam: Yes Swamiji, I wrote them that the books were meant for sales during the Cultural Association Conference.

Swamiji: There you are wrong. It is not for the conference. It is for the sales during the weekly Satsang as per the instructions of Sri A.N. Sharma. Kindly write again mentioning them correctly.

Paripoornam: Yes Swamiji.

It always happens, when we do a particular work correctly Swamiji never even asks whether we have done that work or not. But if we commit any mistake in our work, even though we

don't inform about that work to Swamiji, he somehow understands that we have not done the work properly and catches us
very nicely with his cross-questions within the twinkling of a
second. It is a mystery how Swamiji understands, particularly
when we do mistakes. His, is the Vision of Wisdom, without the
least exertion Swamiji understands things as it is. With this power only, he helps aspirants in the right path, all over the world,
sitting in a remote corner of Rishikesh.

16th MARCH 1959

THE INNER ESSENCE

"Om Namo Venkatesanandaya."

"Om Namo Amaranandaya."

"Satyam Jnanam Anantam Brahma."

This is how Swamiji greets one by one who comes and prostrates before him in his Kutir every-day.

It is not the Form with a Name of Sri Venkatesananda, Swamiji sees, but Lord Venkatesa, he sees.

It is not the person Amarananda or Satyajnanam, Swamiji sees, but SATYA JNANA AMARA ANANDA ATMA, he sees in them.

He has found himself in All, he sees All in himself.

WORRY-LESS MAN

Swami Venkatesanandaji was telling that Sri X. was having some family worries which made him do some unlawful act.

Swamiji: Who is not having worry? Everybody is having some worry or other. A householder is having family worry; a Sannyasi is having his Bhiksha worry. Worriless man verily is the enlightened sage who has controlled his mind, the root-cause of all worries.

THE ETERNAL TRUTH

Sri D.V. Rajan, secretary of the Divine Life Society Branch Calcutta came and prostrated before swamiji.

Swamiji: Is it D.V. Rajan? I couldn't recognise you.

D.V. Rajan: Yes Swamiji. I have undergone two operations which have completely changed my body. That is why Swamiji is not able to recognise me at once.

Swamiji: Don't worry. It is the nature of the body to change. But Atma is changeless, and eternal.

D.V. Rajan: We are trying a separate building for the society, Swamiji, but some obstacles are there, we could not take the work. We don't know what to do?

Swamiji: Wherever there is good intention to do good, obstacles and obstructions come side by side. Don't be discouraged; because victory is sure to come in the end.

NAME: LIFE-TRANSFORMER

After seeing the letters, Swamiji started to the office. Swami Krishnananda Mata, an old lady, who prays daily for her early departure from this world, came and bowed to Swamiji.

Swamiji: Aoo, Mataji, how are you?

Old Lady: Expecting the time to come early, Swamiji. Somehow God is not granting.

Swamiji: All the same to be here or to go there, if Ram Nam is there constantly in the lips.

From this remark, Swamiji gives us the clue how the man can change his daily life into a Divine Life. According to one's Prarabdha, one is placed under particular conditions, environments and status in life. But if one tries to live in the constant remembrance of God, these conditions and environments and status never affect him at all. It is all the same for him who has taken refuge in the Name of the Lord, whether he lives here in this world in a particular condition or in some other world in a different condition.

GOOD AND EVIL

Swamiji was proceeding to the office. Sri Santosh came and told about A's health and consulted about some medicines to be given to her.

Swamiji: Santosh, wherefrom did you get that medicine?

Santosh: From Swami Chidanandaji, Swamiji. He is keeping wonderful medicines with him.

Swamiji: He is a lover of medicines, I think. Santosh, is he not a very compassionate man?

Santosh: Of course Swamiji.

Swamiji: Always look to the good side of men and matters. Even when you come across people who are rude to you, feel that God provides you with a chance to strengthen your mind through him. Always see "what is good" in others, in order to develop, that particular good quality in you.

"See no evil," but if you happen to see any evil, see that evil never comes to you. God created both good and evil in this world for us to learn, from the "good" to be good and from the "evil" to be free from evil. Therefore both good and evil are only good.

THE DIVINE DESCENT

One Srinivasan from Madhurantakam near Madras, met Swamiji on the way. He was having some hesitation to stay permanently in the Ashram. Swamiji also wants him to stay. He prostrated before Swamiji.

Swamiji: Oji! Don't hesitate. Don't fear that you won't get the comforts here. Don't worry, I will supply you even betel leaves and nut for you (Srinivasan is used to the betel leaves chewing.) For your sake I am also going to practise that habit.

Swamiji, in his boundless compassion is ready to come even to the level of an ordinary Sadhak in order to raise him to the heights of spirituality. In the initial stages, one cannot fully realise Swamiji's greatness. So knowing this, he voluntarily comes to an aspirant as a sincere friend who shares everything of the Sadhak, keeping himself in the same level of the person concerned, helps him, suggests him the right path and gradually pulls him to his side and finally lifts him to the heights of Divinity. Such is Siva's compassion.

GOOD AND EVIL—II

After the usual Kirtan and Prayer, in the office, Swamiji was replying to a question put by a lady devotee.

Swamiji: Vices exist in order to glorify virtue. Pride exists in order to glorify humility. Black exists in order to glorify white. Evil exists in order to glorify good. When everybody becomes virtuous how can you ever appreciate virtues at all. Evil is a kind of knowledge to show the superiority of goodness by way of compassion.

DIVINE STOCK-EXCHANGE

A devotee from Chittaranjan brought Badam Halwa (a sweetmeat) to Swamiji. It was distributed immediately and everybody enjoyed it as it was prepared very nicely. Swamiji also enjoyed, not in the sweetness of Badam Halwa, but he enjoyed in the enjoyment of others when they relished the Sweetmeat.

Laughing with those who laugh, and weeping with those who weep, sharing the pain and pleasure of one and all, still keeping the calmness and peace in the heart, without being affected by any external affairs, is the state in which Swamiji, the Enlightened sage, always is.

Turning to the devotee who brought the sweets. He said,

Swamiji: Oji, you have prepared it nicely. You gave me this sweetmeat but I will give you the sweetmeat of wisdom, sweetness of which will be lingering in you eternally.

Such is Swamiji's Infinite Grace to give a valuable everlasting gift in return to a petty offering given with full heart. Describing this quality of Swamiji, it reminded me, Sri

Ramanathan Chettiar's speech today in the office. He put it humorously.

"We are doing an exchange business with Swamiji. We offer only half of our heart, that also half-heartedly, but Swamiji showers on us, in exchange, his grace, his blessings and everything of his which are invaluable and everlasting. So in this "exchange business" Swamiji is the loser."

When Swamiji was returning from the office the same beggar's group who came yesterday, approached Swamiji for money.

Swami Hridayanandaji: Like this they will come daily, Swamiji. Swamiji need not give anything today. They should not be encouraged.

Swamiji: Doesn't matter. God is giving. (Turning to Satchidananda) Oji give them each one rupee.

This is Swamiji's practical way of teaching. his teaching is not merely "Give", but "Give, Give, Give." Everything has been given to you by God only to give and not to keep. Give everything which you get by the grace of God, then you get everything, you give. Sivananda Ashram is a proof for this. No budget. Swamiji goes on giving, giving ceaselessly giving everything, still everything flows like Ganges to his will.

"Om Namo Narayanaya."

Swamiji enters his Kutir.

17th MARCH 1959

YOUR DAILY DIARY

Sri Sushila, a devotee from Delhi, who is a Nurse by profession, met Swamiji with her sister, in his Kutir this morning. After prostration she gave her diary to Swamiji for his autograph with his Blessings.

"Washerman	Rs. 8
House Rent	Rs. 25
Vegetable	Rs. 5
Hotel Account	Rs. 26
Milk Man	Rs. 15

We all wondered what Swamiji was reading from that diary. To the surprise of all, it was only from a blank page of the diary Swamiji was reading all these above things. All burst into laughter.

By this, Swamiji points out that the purpose of maintaining a diary is not to write all about these worldly affairs, as 95% of people do in these days, which is in no way useful to us. Diary should be maintained for the purpose of noting our spiritual progress; the time we have devoted for our prayer, and meditation; our success and failure in achieving the ethical perfection etc....... At the end of every month if we turn and go through the pages, we will be able to know "What we were before", "What we are now at present", and "How we should be in the future." "Keep daily spiritual diary; you will evolve quickly"—This is what Swamiji again and again re-minds us during his Kirtan.

AUTOGRAPH

Then Swamiji inscribed his Immortal Teaching "SERVE,

LOVE, GIVE, PURIFY, MEDITATE, REALISE; BE GOOD; DO GOOD";
in the diary and with his blessings gave it back to Sri Sushila.

Sri Sushila felt a bit difficult to read what Swamiji wrote.
Swamiji helped her and told, Oji Nirmala, try to practise the last
couplet "Be Good, Do Good" and others will join automatically."

Here Swamiji gives us the process of gradual evolution
without any emotional revolution which always ends in "com-
pulsory walkout" altogether from spiritual path itself. If one
tries to "Be Good" and to "Do Good", he has to *"Serve all"* and
"Love all", which naturally *purifies* his heart and makes him fit
for *meditation* which leads to *realisation*. "Be Good, Do Good,
Serve, Love, Purify, Concentrate, Reflect, Meditate, Realise."
This is Sivananda's Spiritual Ladder.

CONQUEST OF ANGER

Swamiji: Sushila, Do you get angry with your patients?

Sushila: No Swamiji. Those who come to me as my patients are all railway officers. So I cannot get angry with them.

Swamiji: That is it ....(turning to Sri Chandravati, the
Rani of Gaya) Chandravati, you will get angry with your servants, is it not so?

(Laughter)

By this Swamiji points out that one can get angry only with
the meek and weak but not with stronger or superior. Inability to
get angry with a person, superior or stronger to you, cannot be
said "Control of Anger." Get angry with anger itself and get
over anger. That is the way for the Conquest of Anger.

Swamiji was coming out of his Kutir followed by disciples
and devotees. Just then we happened to witness a scene on the
road where a lady was going on shouting and quarrelling with a
man, may be her husband. Swamiji humorously remarked, "If

there are ladies with such quarrelsome nature the number of Sannyasins will increase like anything." (All burst into laughter.)

When Swami Raghunath told Swamiji that a lady who is lying down on the way-side near the office, gets angry and shouts when asked to remove her things from that place, Swamiji remarked about this to Sri D.V. Rajan.

What is the use of sitting like this, posing like a Vairagi, and unnecessarily causing disturbance to people. This is not real Vairagya. There was a person in Rama Ashram, who used to sit for hours together in the hot sun and pose like a great Japa Yogi but who used to get angry even for trifling things. Merely sitting in the hot sun, or standing in the water for hours together, taking only fruits and milk, wearing only Kowpeena does not constitute real Vairagya or spirituality. Mere control of body without the control of mind is not at all good. Control of one's lower emotions, lust, anger, greed, hatred—these alone constitute real spirituality.

EMBODIMENT OF GOODNESS

Near the office Swamiji was sitting for the photograph. It was lunch time. Some of the Guest Room boys, standing with the food trays, were hesitating to pass in front of Swamiji. Noticing this, Swamiji called them. "Oji, you can go. Don't wait for me. The food will become cold." Then he checked the tray and was satisfied with the food which was kept there. "Why can't you cover the food with clean tray cloth. Acchaji, Chalo Chalo. Go. Go." Is it merely an inspection or an action, out of motherly affection? How beautifully Swamiji takes care of his devotees and disciples? Who is this Swamiji "mother or father, friend or Guru?" As a mother he feeds us nicely. As a father he reminds us of our duty. As a friend he gives us wise counsel. As a Guru he guides us in the right path and takes us to the Ultimate

Goal. Don't you feel that Swamiji is the embodiment of everything that is good in the world?

THEATRE NURSE'S DUTIES

A lady doctor and her assistant came from Kankhal, to have Swamiji's Darshan in the office. After giving them some books he enquired about the Assistant.

Swamiji: Are you the Assistant Doctor?

Devotee: No Swamiji. I am in-charge of the Operation Theatre. I am assisting during the operations.

Swamiji: What is the important requisite for the one who assists in the operation?

Devotee:..............

Swamiji: "Presence of mind." You must know beforehand the correct instruments which are needed at a particular time during the operation. Suppose you give a wrong instrument by mistake, during the operation if the doctor gets angry, don't' feel upset. Be calm. Be bold. And do the things needed carefully, otherwise you will do more mistakes and the operation won't come out successful.

They thanked Swamiji and took leave. I wonder, is there any field, Swamiji does not know!

During the night Satsang, Sri. Atmaramji was telling Swamiji that he could not listen to the discourse due to the disturbance caused by the persons who were standing outside the Satsang Hall. Swamiji kept silent.

OBSTACLES WITHIN

What is that silence? What is the instruction behind it? That silence impressively instructs you. "O Man, don't wait for the waves to subside, if you really want to have pleasant sea bath. Moreover it is not possible to cover the thorny ground and walk over it. Just wear a pair of shoes, protect yourself and walk boldly. This is the way. This is the truth.

INSTRUCTIONS FOR WRITERS

After Arati Swami gave some constructive suggestions to Santosh, on article writing.

"Santosh, don't break your head for the sake of bringing "Rhyme" in the sentence. If you concentrate on "Rhyme" you cannot bring out correct expression to your thoughts. Always write simple English. The purpose of writing is to make others benefited at least to some extent, when they read it. What is the use of writing multi-compound sentences which no man can understand? Correct expression of thought in simple language makes one a successful writer."

RELIGIOUS UNITY IN PRACTICE

Swamiji, on the way back to his Kutir, was standing near the entrance.

"Om Namo Narayanaya. May Lord bless you Banami Khuda, Mubarak, Sat Nam Ek Omkar, Om Tat Sat."

This is how he takes leave from all devotee who follow him up to his Kutir.

This is Swamiji's practical way of accepting all faiths and all religions reminding us of the "Unity of Religions" and making us realise the essence of all those faiths.

18th MARCH 1959

TRUE GREATNESS OF MAN

The Kutir's door was opened. It was 10 a.m. Swami Venkatesananda, after prostration handed over the typed article written by Swamiji.

Swamiji, 'The Himaya Jyoti' was going through the "HIMAYA JYOTI", the typed article. He turned towards Sri Atmaramji,

Swamiji: Atmaramji, where lies the real greatness of man.

Atmaramji:..........

Swamiji: The real greatness of man lies not in his material comforts, cars, bangalows and bank-balance, but only in the depth of spiritual experience he possesses. There lies the real greatness of man.

THE PATH OF RENUNCIATION

A middle aged young man who has resigned his well paying job in Delhi, came here with the intention of staying in the Ashram, to devote his whole time for spiritual life. He prostrated before Swamiji, and was waiting for his orders. Swamiji started to feel his pulse.

Swamiji: Oji better you go back to Delhi and accept the job. Don't do all these things in emotion. Your wife and children will suffer there. They will come and cry here. Moreover it is very difficult for you to stick in this path.

Aspirant: No Swamiji. I have no inclination to work at all. My family won't suffer there because I have made all arrangements for them. They have two houses and Rs. 5000/- net cash. I have determined to embrace the spiritual life. In any case I will stick to it.

Whoever comes to stay in the Ashram, Swamiji discourages them first, but it is only just to test their determination. Swamiji, here understood that this aspirant has real Vairagya and Mumukshutva.

Swamiji: Acchaji, then what is your intention? What do you want to do?

Aspirant: I want to travel whole of India, visit important shrines and sacred places, sing Lord's Name wherever I go. This is my intention.

Swamiji: Oji it is not an easy task. You have to undergo many difficulties. You won't get food, shelter, etc., in time.

Aspirant: No Swamiji. God will take care of all those things.

Swamiji: That is alright. God will provide you everything. But before that He will see whether you are fit enough for His grace. You have to face many a trial and tribulation. In the midst of all these, you can't think of God and you may even lose faith. Our faith in God is not yet developed to such an extent, to face all the pains and sufferings and think of Him. The best way is, stay here for a month or two, engage yourself in some work for few hours daily and the rest of the time you can meditate.

Aspirant: No Swamiji, I have no interest in any work. I cannot work. I want to utilise the whole time exclusively for meditation.

Swamiji: My dear Sir, go step by step. Don't jump from first to fifth. You will break your legs. It is not possible to meditate all the twenty-four hours for a new aspirant. You can do so for only a few days. Afterwards the mind will put "Automatic Vacuum Break." In the name of meditation you will be only sleeping. It will produce inertia (Tamas). Mind should be controlled tactfully with discrimination. Otherwise like a vicious horse it will throw you down and run away. Few hours meditation, few hours Japa, sometime Kirtan, some Asan, a few rounds of Pranayama, a little Selfless work, combining all these methods you must work out to win over the mind. Then only you will have a harmonious, synthetic development of head, heart and hands. Don't think that work is a hindrance to meditation. On the other hand it is very helpful. The work done selflessly, refreshes the mind which is tired due to the meditation. So don't hesitate. Take up some work and stay here.

Aspirant: Excuse me, Swamiji, I cannot work.

Swamiji: Acchaji. You need not work. You are interested in Kirtan, is it not? Do Akhanda Kirtan for a few hours daily in the Bhajan Hall and help in the Mandir Pooja. Alright. Satyajnanam, give him room, clothes everything. Acchaji you can go. Be cheerful. May Lord bless you.

This is what is called the Supreme, unimaginable, and inexpressible kindness of Swamiji. Even after hearing all his analytical advice, if an aspirant wants to have his own way, Swamiji never hesitates to give him a chance in his own way for he knows it for certain that the aspirant will come in his way after sometime.

CHOOSE, FRIEND!

Sri Sucha Singh, a good Sadhak who was staying in the Ashram for a year wanted to go back to his place for getting a job, came to Swamiji to take leave. Swamiji remarked. "Due to some good Poorva Samskaras God places us in an environment where we can utilise our time in prayer and Sadhana and in the company of holy men. It is due to lack of discrimination one wants to leave such a place and go back. God has given both, intellect and as well as conditions. It is left to you to decide whether to walk in the SREYO MARGA, the path of good which takes you to everlasting happiness or in the PREYO MARGA the path with a pleasant appearance, but which drags you to the ever-rounding cycle of birth and death and leads you to destruction in the end. Turning to Suchasingh, Achaji, may Lord bless you. Keep this money with you for your way expenses. Om Tat Sat."

SANNYAS AND UPASANA

Swamiji was proceeding to the office. (Turning to Swami Krishna, Swamiji's cook, Swamiji asked.)

Swamiji: Krishna Prabhu, you do some Pooja daily?

Krishna: No Swamiji. I don't do all those things. (Sannyasi-complex was reflecting in his face.)

Swamiji: Oh! Oh! because you have become a Sannyasi you think it is all inferior to do Pooja and worship, is it not?

Here Swamiji points out, just because one puts orange robes one should not think he has become Brahman and there is nothing more to do except repeating "Sivoham Sivoham." Not by merely repeating Aham Brahmasmi one becomes Brahman. Even after Sannyasa Ramaswamy remains the same Ramaswami with all the same character and conduct. One has to strive hard to purify his heart by worship, Upasana, Japa, meditation, enquiry, etc. Then only he becomes a perfect Sannyasi.

IRRELIGIOUS MOVEMENTS

In the office when Sri D.V. Rajan was narrating about some evil forces which work against the religion in Tamil Nadu, Swamiji remarked. "Even those negative forces are induced only by God. It is only to make the positive to shine more positively. Evil always brings good in the end."

19th MARCH 1959

BEAR INSULT: BEAR INJURY

Swamiji was sitting in the office, going through his letters. Sri Santosh entered. She complained that a certain person has remarked something sarcastically about her article and that made her feel terribly hurt.

Swamiji: Santosh! why do you care for these sort of things? When are you going to be bold to face all these things? When everybody behaves with you nicely, how can you ever strengthen your will? World is such. What to do? You must patiently bear all these difficulties, keeping your eye always fixed on the goal for which you have come here. Just see, you have allowed a wave to raise to disturb your mental peace. It is going to be vibrating at least for 3 or 4 days and because of this disturbance, you will lose all your mental balance, in all other affairs and dealings. Anyhow, Lord bless you. Take these sweets. Be cheerful. Forget and forgive. Om Namah Sivaya.

Swamiji's method of dealing is something wonderful. He never finds fault with anybody. He says "the world is a vast university. Every bit of thing you experience in this world will teach you a lesson, if you look to it in the correct sense."

THIS IS NOT TRUE VAIRAGYA

Sri Swami X came with letters for Swamiji's signature. Along with it he placed before Swamiji a bit of paper in which he has written some of his needs.

Swamiji: Oji, you need not write it in a paper and give me. Tell me straightaway your wants.

Swami.... : I asked the Secretary, he refused. So I came to you, Swamiji.

Swamiji: That is alright. I will give you some money. You yourself go and get the things.

Swami: No Swamiji. I won't touch money. I want only in kind.

Swamiji: Um. ...Money, you won't touch......at the same time you will fight also there. Is it not?

Swamiji points out here, by his remark, that it is hypocrisy to say that one won't touch money and at the same time desires for everything. This is wrong understanding of Vairagya.

COSMIC IDENTIFICATION

Swamiji was coming back to his Kutir. On the way Swamiji met an Australian tourist, who is staying in the Ashram at present.

"Have you taken your lunch," Swamiji kindly enquired him.

"Yes Thanks. Have you finished yours?" He asked.

"O... Yes." Swamiji told him with a smile and added, "I have taken lunch through all stomachs."

Here is an another occasion. A gem slips out of Swamiji's mouth. It gives us the clue to understand the real Sivananda.

He is the "MAHA KARTA" AND "MAHA BHOKTA," the Great Doer, and the Great Enjoyer. He has realised the Oneness of All within himself. He feels that he works through all hands, sees through all eyes, eats through all mouths, knows through all minds and enjoys through all. He is the Great doer still the Non-doer. He is the Great Enjoyer, still the non-enjoyer. Do you wonder what is this mystery? Yes. It is a mystery. The mystery about SIVANANDA is the mystery of the SELF. Therefore, to know Sivananda really, one should know one-self.

PHYSICIAN, HEAL THYSELF

During the night Satsang P.S. prostrated before Swamiji. He told that he has written a book "India's destiny" and presented a copy to Swamiji.

Swamiji: You have written about India's Destiny? What is your Destiny?

Mr. P.S. My Destiny..........My Destiny.

Swamiji just gave him a sympathetic look and kept quiet.

"Poor Man! you don't know about your own destiny. You are worried about the nation's destiny as if you are going to change it by your will. It has become a fashion nowadays to all "Tom, Dick and Harry" to talk and write about "Nation's Destiny", "World's Future", "Universal Brotherhood", "Cosmic Consciousness", big big terms like this. All are nothing but mere wordy jugglery and fit for nothing. O Man! 'Listen, first is Self-reform and then Social Reform, first Self-purification and then suggestions to others, first unity with your brothers in your house, and then Universal Brotherhood. Take care of yourself first, and the world will take care of itself."

My God! So much was there, the meaning for that ONE SYMPATHETIC LOOK OF SWAMIJI.

After Arati Swamiji returned to his Kutir. Thus ends the day with the BEGINNINGLESS, ENDLESS, CHANGELESS, ACCOUNTLESS, PRICELESS, OVERFLOWING KARUNASAGAR SAT GURU MAHARAJ, in the favourite Slogan of Sri Daulatramji, a sincere Selfless worker of the Ashram. Om Tat Sat.

20th MARCH 1959

COMPLETE CURE

Today morning, unusually Swami Sangeethanandaji came to Swamiji's Kutir with a worried appearance and prostrated before Swamiji. He told that he is terribly worried about his health for he is having symptoms of diabetes.

Swamiji: Oji, Be bold. Be cheerful. Don't worry. Nothing will happen. I will keep Prayer for you.

"Om Triyambakam Yajamahe," "Oji repeat with, me", (All repeated Maha Mrityunjaya Mantra.)

"How are you now, feeling better", Swamiji smilingly asked Sangeethanandaji. (Laughter)

"Ekam Dasam Idly Kenarthan Grigyantham" Swamiji cut jokes in the words of Sangeethanandaji's Sanskrit Language (A language without a single' Sanskrit word) means, "Can I give you ten rupees more for your Idly daily?"

All burst into laughter continuously for five minutes. Sri Sangeethanandaji altogether forgot all the worry about his health and became cheerful and happy.

Swamiji knows well that the origin of disease is not in the body, in most of the cases, but only in the mind. So instead of telling a remedy first for the disease, Swamiji makes the mind of the person concerned cheerful and happy by his witty talks and humorous remarks and makes 75% of the disease disappear. Further, hear what Swamiji says.

"Sangeethanandaji Maharaj! Take 7 or 8 Vilva leaves early in the morning daily. Avoid too much sweets. Reduce taking rice a little. In no time you will become all right. Don't worry. Acchaji. Om Namah Sivaya. You can go now."

45

Now the remaining 25% of the disease will be made alright by following the above instructions of Swamiji.

NOT YET

An old gentleman prostrated before Swamiji, He handed over a chit in which he has asked Swamiji for a private talk with him.

Swamiji just gazed at him and said "Know Thy Self. That is all. No necessity for any private talk"

Visitor: That I have known already, Swamiji. I have studied so many books on Vedanta. For the past one month I am doing regular Sadhana. I have some doubts to be cleared. So.....I asked for private talk.

Swamiji: Do Japa of "OM" constantly. Meditate that "OM" is everything. OM is Immortality. Om is Infinity. OM is the essence, underlying all these phenomena. All your doubts will be cleared. (After a while) If someone comes and beats you, you must keep quiet. Are you surprised? Yes, that is the Vedantic Test of Non-Dual Reality. That is the yardstick to measure one's Vedantic Anubhava (Experience)

Some may think, that Swamiji gives interview only to big big persons and not for real Sadhaks. It is a cent percent wrong view. There is a peculiar complex in most of the aspirants. They read one or two Vedantic texts, sit for sometime daily gazing at the rafters with all kinds of thoughts, imagining it for deep contemplation on the All-pervading Absolute and then approach holy men and saints and ask them all sort of silly questions, thinking as if they are standing just one or two inches below the transcendental consciousness. Swamiji knows this well and He discourages such persons for any private talk and if at all he does it, it is only due to the infinite Grace and boundless compassion for the aspirants to show them the right path to make them have right understanding, marching the right way towards the Ultimate Goal.

HOW TO AVOID QUARREL

Swamiji heard some heated discussions going on between two persons, when he was sitting in the office. he smilingly remarked "What is the next step.......from vituperation to blows......."What one should do now to avoid it at this very moment. Best thing is, stitch the mouth, put off the mind, cooly walk out from the spot. Sit calmly. Drink a cup of cold water."

What wonderful, practical hints for spiritual Sadhaks to control the anger, Swamiji gives!

21st MARCH 1959

VIDYA MUST GENERATE VINAYA

No visitors could be found in the Kutir today as Swamiji started a bit early to the office.

A Brahmachari from Hardwar, Shantananda by name had Swamiji's Darshan in the office. He was well-versed in Sanskrit language. Swamiji introduced him to Sri Swami Narayananandaji who is also studying for "Vyakarana." In this connection Swamiji remarked.

Swamiji: Sanskrit learning, in most of the cases develops only pride and egoism.

One should not think, Swamiji discourages the learning of Sanskrit. On the other hand in all his writings he insists everyone to learn Sanskrit for it contains the sublime Truths of the LIFE, the LIFE AFTER DEATH, THE LIFE BEYOND LIFE AND DEATH. Swamiji by his above remark, condemns only the after-effects of Sanskrit study in most of the cases. Sanskrit learning should make a person become more humble and simple. An illiterate man without pride and egoism is a thousand times better than a very learned person with egoism and pride.

PRAGMATIC OBEDIENCE

"Shantanandaji, listen. I will tell you a nice story," Swamiji smilingly said. The whole office turned towards Swamiji's side to listen the story.

"There was a Guru" Swamiji started, "He had a very nice disciple; very obedient; takes Master's words as Veda Vakya. The Guru called his disciple one day and said "Sishya, kindly collect some fuel and bring here."

"Kindly pardon me Gurudev. I am not feeling well. So…….." the disciple replied.

"Achhaji, Don't worry. Doesn't matter" the Guru said.

A few days after the Guru again called his disciple.

"Sishya Bhagavan, kindly go to the river and get some drinking water," the Guru asked his disciple.

"Sat Guru Deva, Parama Dayalo, I am ever at your service: but I have a sprain on my left leg I couldn't walk."

This is disciple's reply.

Like this whenever the Guru called him for some work the disciple avoided it with some kind of excuse or other.

Like this whenever the Guru called him for some work the disciple avoided it with some kind of excuse or other.

One day Guru called his disciple "My dear disciple, I have prepared some Halwa and kept it for you. Kindly go and take it." The Guru told him.

"Apka Ajnaji Maharaj! Now how long can I disobey you Maharaj? I am anxiously waiting every moment to obey your orders, My Lord!" The disciple replied and finished the whole Halwa within a moment.

(All burst into laughter.)

How do you like this disciple. Do you know? This is called "EXPLICIT DEVOTION AND IMPLICIT OBEDIENCE" to the Master. (Laughter.)

In this connection Swamiji told about a letter written by a devotee two days back. The letter reads:

Swamiji, a week back I came to your Ashram at about 2-30 p.m. with the intention of having the Darshan of my most beloved Gurudev, and knocked the Kutir's door. I was disappointed; nobody opened the door, or even replied me. I felt, if Gurudev hurts the feelings of disciple like this, where can the disciple go for consolation. Therefore, I have determined to fast unto death if I don't get a satisfactory explanation from Gurudev within 4 days."

Swamiji smilingly remarked "see, how many varieties you find in this world! Do you call this devotion. This is nothing but a childish adamancy. Anyhow I am going to write only after two days. Let him fast at least for two days. That will do him good and purify him. (All laughed.)

MY DISCIPLE

Swamiji was glorifying his disciples to one of the devotees who was sitting there in front of him.

"This is Swami A. Tamil Chronicler, writer, poet, artist, accountant and what not."

"This is Swami S. Chronicler, poet, Kirtanist, Typist."

"This is Swami H. eye-surgeon, poet, author of four books. All kinds of varieties are here.

Just at this time Swamiji saw the face of those persons whom he glorified. Perhaps he would have noted that "Sriman Egoism" was peeping through their eyes, suddenly he turned to the devotee. "Bhuvaji, do you want thieves also here. Within one second they will even take my head away." Such persons also are there (All burst into laughter.)

This is Swamiji's S.B. 40 injection to weaken the power of Sriman "Egoism." Doctors may wonder. "what is this S.B. 40 injection. We have never heard." But very sorry I cannot say what it is. Because it is a secret. Swamiji alone, has got the Trade Right for that medicine. He alone knows when to use that medicine, because he is the doctor of doctors.

"Do you want to know what is S.B. 40. It is secret. Keep it with you. Don't say it to anybody. S.B. 40 means shoe-beating 40."

22nd MARCH 1959

THE ALL-SEEING EYE

The heavy flow of visitors and devotees from all over India, in Swamiji's Kutir today, when it was opened, indicated us the arrival of summer season.

Swamiji's Kutir was "house full." One by one the devotees came and prostrated before Swamiji and took their seats. Sri Santosh brought some of her friends for Swamiji's Darshan.

Santosh: Swamiji, this gentleman wants to have a private talk with you.

Swamiji: Private Talk! All must go out from here then, except myself and that person, is it not so?

(Laughter)

Even God also should not be there??!!

(Laughter)

Swamiji by this remark points out that one cannot hide anything from God for He is everywhere and at all times. Even if one goes and does something underground, God is there always watching his action. Why only action? He is the very witness of our thoughts even. Here it reminds us of a story, Swamiji has written in one of his books.

'Once a Guru wanted to test his disciples. He called them and gave them each a fruit and asked them to eat it where no one can see. One disciple went to the interior forests and ate it thinking none had watched his action. The other disciple came back to his Guru and told "Gurudeva, there is no place where none can see my action because God is watching me always and everywhere."

"Therefore be honest, be sincere, be truthful."

51

LIFE-TRANSFORMING LECTURES

Sri Subramanya Bhuva, a Hatha Yogi and a staunch devotee of Swamiji told that some of his friends who had no belief in God or Religion, were entirely changed when they heard Swamiji's appealing lectures and inspiring songs "Eat a Little Drink a Little" and "Song of eighteen Ities" during their ALL-INDIA TOUR in 1950, at Trichi in South India.

The reason is, one should understand that Swamiji's writings and lectures are not merely the vomiting of the "mugged-up" scriptures, like some of the so-called, dry philosophers these days. His writings and lectures are the very expressions of his INNER EXPERIENCE. They are the outpourings from the inner store of his HEART CORE. There is life in his every word and in every sentence, He writes and talks. So they go straight into the heart of a person, destroys all the barriers that the impure mind puts on the way. So there is no wonder, what Bhuvaji said, that even the atheist were entirely changed, when they heard Swamiji's lectures.

APPROACH TO SIVANANDA

Swamiji turned towards Santosh "Santosh, your sister has sent money to construct a Kutir. Where do you like it?

Santosh: What is 'your liking' Swamiji?

Swamiji: I cannot LIKE anything without your LIKING.

Here Swamiji shows us two methods by which we can approach Him.

"God likes and grants always that which you like and ask for. You cannot simply keep quiet expecting God to help you. You have to sincerely aspire for a thing and work for it, then God comes to your help according to your aspiration and faith. This is the method, common to most of the aspirants.

But there is higher state also where the devotee keeps no

liking at all whatsoever for himself. He keeps quiet with firm conviction and staunch belief that everything in this world moves only according to God's liking and God's will. This is what is called SELF-SURRENDER. In such case God never waits for the devotees' liking. He automatically takes care of his devotee who has already surrendered his individual will.

Similar is the case with Swamiji. If you are an aspirant of the first type, Swamiji waits for your Iiking in everything and fulfils accordingly. If you are of the latter type, where you surrender to Swamiji completely, Swarniji himself takes care of you in everything and does everything for your good.

INTELLECT: YOUR FRIEND AND FOE

In the Office Sri D.V. Rajan told about a well-known person in South India. He said "He is very learned, good writer, poet, research scholar, politician, and very intelligent......but......... .with no faith in God or religion."

Swamiji: What is the use of this kind of intelligence? INTELLECT should become an INSTRUMENT to lead one to INTUITION. Otherwise INTELLECT becomes an interruption to one's EVOLUTION. Perverted intellect is not intelligence.

Sri Ramaswami, Dy. Minister of Rlys., Sri Ambujammal, a great social worker and President of the famous Srinivasa Gandhi Nilayam, Sri Jeyalakshmi, Director of Women's Welfare Board, Madras, all joined together have come to see Swamiji. Swamiji took them to the Eye Hospital. Dr. Hridayananda, showed them all, the operated cataract lenses. When they were watching, Swamiji remarked humorously but instructively "Now have you seen this lens? This opaque lens hides only the vision of the eye. But the small eye lens hides the Real and makes the world appear attractive."

Here Swamiji points out how the eyes can cheat a person, show him a wrong as right, an ugly thing as attractive one, the

Unity as diversity, and so on. So one should first control the senses which lead to the control of mind which in turn leads to the cognition of the ONE, the REAL.

INTROVERSION

Sri Ambujammal: Swamiji, one of my eyes has gone out of use. I cannot see anything outside properly.

Swamiji: (with a smile) I also cannot see anything outside.

Here Swamiji gives us the difference in Vision, between a wise man and an ordinary man. If an ordinary person cannot see anything outside means it is due to the defect in his eyes. Is it the same case with Swamiji also? Is it because of that he says, "he could not see anything outside"? No. No. Certainly not. What is there for Swamiji to see outside, something different from his own Self. He could not see anything outside because he sees nothing besides Atman which is within himself and outside also. That is why he said, He could not see anything outside, WITH A SMILE.

THE OCEAN OF COMPASSION

There was a grand Pada Puja today by the Rani of Nepal. After the Abhisheka usually the devotee, who does Pada Puja used to stand up and garland Swamiji. Here, the Rani is weak. The garland was given to her. She could not get up and garland Swamiji as she is too weak to stand even. To the surprise and astonishment of one and all, Swamiji, to whom Governors, Ministers and Maharajas come all the way to Rishikesh to prostrate and get his blessings BENT DOWN and accepted the garland Himself from her hands.

My pen stops writing. My mind has become blank. I don't know how to measure the ocean with a small cup! How to describe the indescribable compassion of Swamiji?

SELF-JUSTIFICATION

During the night Satsang a devotee brought some sweet cakes. They were distributed immediately. An orthodox Pandit who used to come to Swamiji often, to get some financial help, was also sitting there. The cake was given to him. Swamiji noticed him enjoying the cakes nicely.

Just for joke Swamiji told, "Panditji Bhagavan, Is Me Anda Hai, Math Khana, (means they have added egg in it. So don't take it)." Panditji replied, "Doesn't matter Swamiji Maharaj. This is Swamiji's Prasad. So I don't mind."

Swamiji: It clearly shows that you like eggs. Why bring an excuse in the name of 'Prasad'

Swamiji instructs us here. "If you are unable to give up certain forbidden acts or if you like certain forbidden things to do, boldly accept it. Instead of that if you justify yourself by bringing some excuse or other in the name of God or Guru and thereby try to hide your weakness it is mere hypocrisy and nothing else. Be frank and be straightforward in all your dealings.

23rd MARCH 1959

SPIRITUALISED MATERIAL LIFE

Sri Om Prakash, a young gentleman friend of Sri Suri a devotee of Swamiji, from Delhi came to the Kutir this morning. Swamiji enquired about him.

Swamiji: Om Prakashji, what is your ambition, to get a job or to start a business?

Om Prakash: I want to do some business, Swamiji.

Swamji: That is good. Start a good business. Work hard. Earn four or five lakhs of rupees. Then stop that business and start business with God. Business with God is very profitable. Because your investment is only a little selfless service, a little prayer, a little Japa and meditation. The profit you gain out of it, is everlasting peace and eternal happiness.

Swamiji never advises anybody to embrace spirituality all on a sudden, without giving any consideration for men's inclination to enjoy the life in the world. "Stay in your own home, do your duties and fulfil your responsibilities in life. Side by side, at the same time, you can grow in spirituality also. Then a time will come when you will be able to utilise all your time in the constant meditation on the Supreme, leaving aside all the cares and worries of the world."

This is the spiritualised material life best suited to the modern man of this Sputnik Age as propounded by Sri Swami Sivananda, the Twentieth Century saint.

SIVA'S KINDNESS

A devotee from Calcutta wants to give a Bandara to all the inmates of the Ashram on 24th. Swami Vasudevananda came and told Swamiji in the office, that it is not possible to have the Bandara on that day, as it is going to be a lunar eclipse day.

Swamiji said "Oji we should not stop it on any account. All the way he has come from Calcutta for this purpose. He wants it on the same day and if he hears this he will feel for it. What does it matter if there is lunar eclipse. It comes only in the dead of night when everybody sleeps. So we have to do it on any account. He will be pleased much.

Swamiji's kindness is such, he will go out of the way to please a sincere devotee somehow or other. He never bothers and also bears, even if it causes some inconvenience to him or to his Ashram.

24th MARCH 1959

CHARITY WHILE YET ALIVE

Swamiji was returning to his Kutir after the office work. On the way a Sindhi lady from Nyasaland, (Pr. E. Africa) just coming to the Ashram, approached Swamiji in a desperate condition, caught hold of Swamiji's Feet and wept.

It was told that she lost her husband a few months ago.

The Darshan of Swamiji, The Holy One, made her peaceful. Then Swamiji took her to his Kutir, consoled her, gave her Mantra for Japa, and conducted prayers for the departed Soul. The saintly Presence of Swamiji made her absolutely calm and quiet within a moment. She presented Swamiji, a Persian carpet and offered hundred rupees for feeding Sadhus and Mahatmas, of the Ashram, went away with a peaceful mind.

Swamiji remarked, "Charitable nature comes usually to rich men only after death and not before."

Swamiji instructs us, that we should develop charitable nature even while yet alive. Then it adds to our good merits not only here in this world but also helps hereafter in the onward journey of the soul.

Swamiji says, "Be like a cow, giving milk while it is alive and not as a pig which gives its flesh for eating after it is dead."

25th MARCH 1959

DETACH ATTACH

Delhi devotees have utilised their "HOLY" holidays in the company of Swamiji, the Holy One. The Kutir was filled with the devotees from Delhi, today,

Sri Ramakrishna from the Central Secretariat New Delhi with Dr. Sri Guruswamy came and prostrated before Swamiji.

After his kind enquiry, Swamiji, pointing to Sri Atmaram told Ramakrishna.

"Ramakrishna, see! he has succeeded before you can. He has thrown away everything, settled here and spends his time in Japa, Satsang and meditation. Whereas you have not determined yet, worrying about so many things."

Swamiji here tells us that one, who has sincere and intense aspiration for Divine Life need not wait for fulfilling all the worldly responsibilities in life as they are endless. Maya's powerful hands will drag him in some guise. Therefore the Sadhaka with strong will should throw aside everything and, devote his life for spirituality exclusively.

WHERE TO STAY?

Ravindar, an emotional type of aspirant who thinks himself fit for Raja Yoga Sadhana asked Swamiji for a comfortable secluded room where he could stay and practise Raja Yoga.

Swamiji: You want a comfortable room. You should be able to do Sadhana anywhere! The whole world is your house. So stay wherever you like and try to do Sadhana.

Swamiji never encourages an aspirant who wants to lead an easy-going comfortable life. He knows well, such an aspirant cannot do any Sadhana in such circumstances. He expects the Sadhaka to undergo hardships in life so that he gets experience which develops his Will strong, to face the adverse conditions in spiritual path.

ADVICE TO A SANNYAS CANDIDATE

Just then Sri Anantanarayan, a sincere aspirant from Delhi, who wants to take Sannyas Diksha from Swamiji came with his father and prostrated. His father told Swamiji that his son should not be given Sannyas till his mother's death, for, he said, that his mother would feel upset to see her only son in Sannyas garb.

Swamiji: Anantanarayan, I think what your father says is correct. Stay here. Do your Sadhana. Write letters now and then to your mother. Once a year you can go and stay with her for some days. Let her not feel in her last days due to the separation of her son. Let her have a peaceful end. Then, you can embrace Sannyasa. Don't worry. Even now you are a Sannyasi. Sannyasa lies not only in the cloth. Then Swamiji praised his father for his boldness in giving consent for his son's Sannyasa Diksha cheerfully.

Both the father and son were satisfied and left the place.

Swamiji is a master psychologist. He gives hope to two different feelings of two different persons, simultaneously, and makes them both feel that Swamiji is on their side.

HOLY SCENES ON "HOLY" DAY

Swamiji emerged out from his Kutir. There stand the "Happy Holy Mass" waiting for Swamiji's Darshan outside the Kutir.

"Bolo Sat Guru Maharaj Ki Jai" the crowd shouted.

"Satchidananda, give them twenty-five rupees Swamiji said.

A few yards he proceeds. A snake charmer comes to Swamiji and bows.

"Satchidananda, five rupees." The Snake Charmer goes with a happy smile.

Swamiji further goes some distance. O there stands a man with two monkeys. He makes the monkeys salute Swamiji.

"Oji give him three rupees."

Like this till he reached his office he was going on giving.

EMBODIMENT OF JOY AND BLISS

Office was overflowing with devotees. Swamiji's table was overflowing with fruits and sweets. Devotees' hands were overflowing with the latest books and magazines, Swamiji gave them. Joy was over flowing in the face of "OVER-FLOWING KARUNA SAGAR" Sat Guru Maharaj.

Sri Santosh entered the office. When she was bowing to Swamiji Sri Brij Mohini sprinkled the coloured powder on her face. Santosh got terribly hurt and she blurted out, "I don't like these things, Swamiji—I never play with anybody and so no-body I like to play with me also."

Swamiji: (with a naughty smile) Oji Brij Mohiniji, don't do it for the second time.

My goodness! the whole crowd burst into laughter.

"Santosh, this orange looks at you. Take it." Swamiji said with a smile. Santosh took it and left the office with a pleasant mood.

How is it possible for any one to keep an angry face in the presence of Swamiji the embodiment of joy and bliss. Within a moment He will make a "castor oil face" in a "glaxo baby's face."

SIVA'S GRACE

Someone brought some saltish preparations. Swamiji kept

some in his hand and called Sri Atmaram who was sitting in the front.

"Atmaramji, come here, this is for you."

Sri Atmaram got up so anxiously and came to Swamiji. Suddenly Swamiji put it in his own mouth and cheated him. (All enjoyed the joke.) After some time he called him again and cheated him in the same way. When Swamiji called Atmaram for the third time, he was hesitating, thinking that Swamiji will cheat him this time also. To his surprise Swamiji gave him the whole lot.

Atmaram: Swamiji, I thought this time you will cheat me.

Swamiji: I cheated you twice, only in order to give you the whole lot.

When God wants to shower his Grace on his devotee abundantly, He creates a situation in which the devotee feels, that he has lost everything, and makes him feel that he is helpless. This makes him surrender to God completely. Then He showers his grace abundantly to the surprise of the devotee.

Similar is the case with Sivananda, who is not only My God, but your God and everybody's God.

WORLD IS UNREAL

Miss Martha Nett, an American disciple entered and bowed to Swamiji. She couldn't get a place to sit. She was standing behind the bench. "Miss Nett, kindly sit down in the chair" Swamiji said. She gave an enquiring look at Swamiji because she couldn't find any chair nearby. "Sit on the imaginary chair. After all the whole world is nothing but imagination" Swamiji said with a smile. (Laughter)

This is a sarcastic humorous hit to the lip-Vedantins who do all sorts of unwanted things and justify their weakness by saying "after all the world is unreal."

WHO AM I?

Dr. Hridayanandaji wrote something in a paper and gave it to Sri Santananda, who was standing in front of Swamiji. Swamiji noticed this and asked "What is that you have written." "I noted what Swamiji talked a few minutes ago" Hridayananda replied.

"A few minutes back—'What I talked' ...I myself don't know." Swamiji said.

Swamiji, the Sahaja Jnani is ever fixed in the Self even though he appears to be talking, eating and acting. He acts and talks spontaneously without any effort. So he is not conscious of his acts or talks. "Gunaa Guneshu Vartante" "Senses move amidst sense-objects" that is what the Gita describes the state of a Sahaja Jnani. He never bothers about what is done by him and what is not done by him for he identifies himself with the Self, the non-doer, the witness of all actions and thoughts.

"SWAN-LIKE" SIVA

"Whose kerchief is this." Sri D. V. Rajan was shouting. Someone has left his kerchief on the bench.

"Doesn't matter, you keep it. (Laughter.) Once left, once for all left." Swamiji remarked.

After few minutes the owner came and took his kerchief.

Swamiji: Oji if something drops from your pocket, think God wants it to give to someone who is in need of it. So don't pick it again and put it in your pocket. When you take food, some eatables fall down, don't take it. Leave it for some creature.

The devotee agreed and left.

Swamiji is like a swan in one way, which separates the milk from the water. Similarly Swamiji separates the "good" in all the matters. The Swan takes the milk for itself, but Swamiji, never takes the "good" for himself, but gives the "good" to others.

AS THE HEART SO THE ACTION

Just then a visitor with his family came for Swamiji's Darshan without any previous intimation about his arrival. After his kind enquiry Swamiji asked Shantananda to give them lunch. Shantananda was hesitating as it was past lunch hour and the food also was over. Noticing this Swamiji said.

"Doesn't matter. Take them. Manage somehow. Give them some curd, pappad and some fruits."

Shantananda, took them to the Guest Room.

Swamiji remarked:

"Even if you are unable to give, at least talk nicely. Unless you are in your heart how are you going to be nice in your actions."

"To be good in actions is to be good in heart, because actions are the expressions of one's thoughts. The external action does not matter much because one's actions will only be according to "What one is in his heart." Therefore be good in order to do good." Thus points out Swamiji by his remark.

Swamiji started back to his Kutir after Kirtan. "Ramachandra Raghu Vira" Kirtan by Swamiji in the end was very emotional and soul-stirring. The whole crowd followed the Kirtan.

Sri Rudrani Senon approached Swamiji. She said "Swamiji I have dropped my keys somewhere. I found it afterwards from the road. Now am I to keep it or throw it?"

Swamiji: Oji I told, only money and food should not be taken back, if once it is dropped. So you can keep the key with you.

Swamiji points out here that one should not follow the teachings of Guru with an incorrect understanding.

"Tattwamasi" "Om Shanti" "May Lord bless you."

Swamiji enters his Kutir.

SIVANANDA LEELA

The whole function today reminded me the theory of evolution.

Swamiji is the Absolute, Brahman here. The Absolute was ONE in the beginning in Its pristine (purity and silence.)

Swamiji also was One in his Pristine Purity and Silence when He was in his inner apartment of his Abode of Bliss.

Then the Absolute joins with the Qualities. There It is in an Unmanifested State.

Then Swamiji comes to the outer varandha of his Kutir and there joins HIM, Sri Hridayananda, Satchidananda and Sri Venkatesananda. Still He is in an unmanifested state.

Then the Absolute Wills. Names and Forms appear. It enters in every form and illumines them.

Here also, the devotees and disciples (Names and Forms) one by one appear before Him. He expands Himself, enters in everybody, (illumines) and inspires them.

The Names and Forms move and act in the Light of the Absolute. Here the devotees and disciples talk and act, do everything, in the Illumined Presence of the Master.

THE ONE BECOMES MANY

Here also Swamiji acts through Many. Then the Lila of Creation starts.

Then Swamiji comes out with his Whole creation, the devotees and disciples. Service, Kirtan, Japa, meditation and varieties of activities are done by Swamiji through the Many.

The involution begins now. Swamiji comes back to his Kutir. Devotees and disciples leave Him outside the entrance. He withdraws himself now. Enters in his abode of Peace, Bliss and Silence and Rest once again in Silence, as ONE in his Inner Apartment.

Om Tat Sat

26th MARCH 1959

AS THE EFFECT SO THE CAUSE

There was a sudden change of chill weather today. Swamiji's long coat which was weeping in the Bureau from the separation of its Master since the summer started, felt very much happy and proud, because it had a chance of adoring the Master.

Sri Guru Bakshi Ram from Delhi with his family prostrated before Swamiji.

Pointing to the young boy, Swamiji said, "I think this boy has devotion".

"No Swamiji, my daughter has very much devotion," the lady replied.

"That is right. As is the effect so should be the cause" Swamiji remarked.

Swamiji says that the upbringing of the child is entirely left in the hands of the mother. As is the mother, the cause, so is the child, the effect. The mother can make a child either as a "Herbert Spencer" or as a heir of the ancient seers. If the mother trains herself in the devotional practices, automatically it induces devotion in the child also.

THE DUTIES OF HUSBAND AND WIFE

Swamiji turned towards Sri Guru Baksh Rai. "What is the duty of a husband?"

Swamiji himself replied: "The husband should take care of the family. He should be a companion to his wife in the life's journey. He must be a husband to his wife till he gives birth to one or two children and then he should become the spiritual friend to his wife and guide her in the spiritual path. Turning towards the lady Swamiji said,

"The wife must be honest and sincere to her husband. She must share the pleasure and pain with her husband. She must induce him and be a help in the devotional practices. She must bring her children as spiritual heroes. She must induce devotion to God in her children."

Both husbands and wife were very much pleased and took leave of Swamiji.

MOUNA OF THE WORLDLY-MINDED

Sri Atmaramji entered the Kutir, came quiet and sat on the sofa. Swamiji asked him whether he is observing Mouna.

He said, "No."

Then Swamiji told, "Do you know when the worldly people observe Mouna......When they are angry."

Swamiji instructs us that Mouna is not the silence of speech leaving the mind with all sorts of thoughts.

Silence of the mind is the real silence.

Mind, full of good and noble thoughts, is said to be always in silence.

WHEN DOCTORS DIFFER

Dr. Kar from Bijnore, a staunch devotee of Swamiji, came to the office for Darshan. Swamiji wanted to call Sri Maj. Gen. Sharma who is staying at present in the Ashram, as both the doctors know each other well.

"Oji call Sharmaji, ..."

Swamiji said and added smilingly,

"When doctors join together diseases increase."

(Laughter)

This is Swamiji's remark on some of the modern doctors who make much of confusion and make the patient puzzled altogether by their diagnosis. Each doctor says something and the patient collapses, not by disease, but out of fear.

Swamiji often used to say "with one doctor there is prescription, with two there is consultation, with three there is cremation." Similar is in the spiritual field also. "With one Guru one gets illumination. With two there is mental confusion. With three one gets admission in the mental hospital.

THE REAL ECZEMA

Sri Sharmaji came and had an interesting talk with Swamiji on the 'Eradication of Malaria'. A person came in the midst and was boring Swamiji for some book which has gone out of stock. Swamiji somehow satisfied and sent him away. Turning to Sharmaji, Swamiji said,

"Sharmaji, What is 'eczema'?"

"Eczema is a skin disease" Sharmaji replied. Swamiji interrupted and said:

"No, No. A person who bores you with his talk or with unnecessary demands is the real eczema. Eczema constantly irritates only the skin, whereas this eczema irritates the mind and tests your patience". (All burst into laughter).

SWAMIJI'S METHOD OF INITIATION

A person prayed to Swamiji for Mantra Diksha. Swamiji called him.

"Come here—what Mantra do you want?" "Rama Mantra, Swamiji," the person replied.

"Acchaji, repeat with me.....Om Sri Ramaya Namah—Om Sri Ramaya Namah—Om Sri Ramaya Namah. Om Tat Sat. May Lord bless you".

Mantra Diksha was over.

People think, Mantra Diksha means, taking a person inside

the room, covering his face, whispering the Mantra in his ears after some Pooja, etc. It need not be so in the case of Swamiji. His is the powerful Master Mind so much so he can switch off his mind completely at will from any external disturbances, in a twinkling of a second and focus all his spiritual force on a particular subject matter on hand, at any time. One can watch, Swamiji keep the Japa Mala in his hands for few minutes with closed eyes, during the initiation when he transmutes his spiritual vibrations to the Mala and as well to the devotee's heart. So one gets maximum benefit out of it, even if it is done in the midst of crowd. Moreover in this busy world when man has no time even to take his food, it is impossible for him to wait for such kind of initiations with Pooja, etc. So Swamiji follows the Easy, Quick but MOST EFFECTIVE method. Moreover Swamiji cannot spare so much time for the sake of one person, for, one has to guide so many thousands of Sadhaks all over the world.

Therefore doubt not, hesitate not, O friends! Come and drink the elixir of Sivananda and enjoy the eternal Bliss.

27th MARCH 1959

EMPTY YOURSELF

Sri Narayanan the manager of Raymon Circus, met Swamiji in his Kutir this morning. After prostration he offered some money to Swamiji. One by one, currency notes, he was taking out from his purse. Swamiji smilingly said:

"Empty it, Sir, then only it will be filled."

Swamiji instructs us to empty, not only our moneypurse but also the mind with its Samskaras collected in innumerable births. Moreover if you empty your purse it will be filled only with perishable wealth, but if you empty your heart, it will be filled with the immortal wealth of Atma which is everlasting peace and eternal Bliss.

PRIVATE INTERVIEW

An American aspirant who arrived just then in the Ashram with the intention of learning Yoga, approached Swamiji and asked:

"Can I have a private talk with you—Swamiji."

Swamiji with a hearty smile replied,

"O Yes! You can have it—in the Heart."

By his remark Swamiji says "Pray sincerely with one-pointed devotion in your heart. There I meet you privately."

Sitting in their home, thousands of miles away sincere and silent prayers done by those aspirants were heard, answered and fulfilled by Swamiji from the remote corner of Rishikesh.

The reason is, they have their private talk with Swamiji in their hearts where alone resides the REAL SIVANANDA.

DEVOTEE'S DOUBTS DISPELLED

Sri M.A. Naidu from South Africa prayed to Swamiji to clear some of his doubts. He asked:

"Why good people suffer in this world, Swamiji?"

Swamiji replied:

"Suffering prepares a man to face adverse condition boldly. Suffering induces endurance and strengthens the will. Pain is a blessing in disguise. When God wants to shower His Grace on a devotee He gives suffering to that person to purify his heart to receive His Grace. You all would have heard the story where Krishna blesses a rich man to become more rich, and curses a poor devotee to lose even the cow, his only possession. When enquired Krishna replied that the devotee's only distraction from the Lord was that cow. So if it is withdrawn He would turn towards Me completely. Therefore, God gives suffering to good people, you understand now?"

Sri Naidoo: Why there are so many religions, Swamiji? Each one says "Follow my path; then only you will reach the goal." Why it is so?

Swamiji: Religion does not say so. Only the selfish persons who claim sole monopoly over religion twist and distort the Truth for their selfish ends. Either Buddha or Sankara or Ramakrishna never said that their path alone is correct.

Sri Naidoo was pleased very much with Swamiji's answer.

Swamiji added again, "Your doubts are cleared now. Is it not? Then the next thing to do is to sit and do Japa and attain Samadhi."

Swamiji insists that one should not simply study the scriptures and teachings of great saints just for curiosity's sake. One should try to follow and put them into practice. Then only they will be benefited.

28th MARCH 1959

THE MODERN PROPHET

Swamiji's voice was recorded in the magnetic tape this morning, in his Kutir. Sri Chandravati with her family and friends came there with her tape-recorder.

All were sitting in front of Swamiji. Swamiji was lying down in the easy-chair. Turning to Sri Bal Badhra an advocate friend of Chandravati's family, Swamiji said:

"Advocate Saheb, plead for the poor, free at least once in a month. This is the Yoga for you." Sri Bal Bhadra agreed to it.

If at all modern people are convinced and accept Swamiji's teachings, it is because of Swamiji's method of expression of the ancient teachings as suited to the taste and temperament of the modern man.

According to Swamiji's teaching, an advocate can practise Yoga as an advocate, by converting his own profession as a means to spiritual attainment.

Similarly a doctor can practise Yoga as a doctor making his own profession as an aid to his spiritual upliftment.

That is why, Swamiji is "The Modern World Prophet" in the words of Sri K.S. Ramaswamy Sastrigal.

SIVA'S SPIRITUAL CHILDREN

Sri Jagat Kishore, the brother-in-law of Sri Chandravati was telling Swamiji that they were hearing the "Chidren's programme" in the tape recorder, in which Swamiji's teachings for children have been recorded a few days back.

"How do you like it?.. .... Nice!!" Swamiji asked.

"Yes Swamiji. Very nice. But, it is, not only for children but......." Jagat Kishore replied.

Swamiji interrupted and said "Yes, for moustached children also."

(All laughed)

Swamiji's "Divine Life for Children" is, meant not only for children, but also for the bodily grown up spiritual children. In the Adhyatmic world intellectual giants are considered as spiritual children!

Similarly Swamiji's "Gita for the Blind" is not for the eyeless ones, but it is meant for those who are blind due to "I"-ness in their heart.

THE NATURE OF TRUE DEVOTION

Swamiji was seeing the letters. One girl student has praised Swamiji in her letter as she has come out successful in her examination.

Swamiji: Suppose she fails, will she abuse me?

(Laughter)

Thus Swamiji imparted to us the secret of true devotion. Devotion developed with the expectation of any selfish motive is not real devotion. In that case devotion loses its value. Devotion should be for devotion's sake and not for any thing else. Such devotion, if developed, leads the aspirant to Self-Illumination quickly.

BHAKTI AND MUKTI

Sri Ramkrishna, Deputy Direceter General of Postal Services had Swamiji's Darshan in the office. A pious and devoted soul, he comes after so many years for Swamiji's Darshan. He knows Swamiji for the past 15 years when he was as a Superintendent of post office in Dehradun. Swamiji entertained him nicely and enquired about his promotion as Director General.

"I want only your Kripa, Swamiji," he replied.

"Yes, Yes. But Grace will come in two forms. One is Bhukti and the other is Mukti," Swamiji replied.

"But I want only Mukti, Swamiji," he said.

"Even if you don't want it, it will come. Charity, generosity, and purity, if a man possesses, they automatically bring forth Bhukti here and Mukti in the end."

He took leave of Swamiji after photograph.

THE PATH AND THE GOAL

"May I ask you a question, Swamiji?" the voice came from a visitor who was standing near the door. "Welcome Sir!" Swamiji's smiling look said so. "What is religion and what is soul?"

"Religion shows the way to soul," Swamiji replied.

"What is the difference between them?" again the visitor asked.

"Religion is the royal road. Soul is the ultimate goal."

The visitor thanked Swamiji and coolly walked out.

RELIGION AND SCIENCE

Swamiji was explaining to a science student. "Science is not against religion. On the other hand science is an aid to religion. Both science and religion search for Truth. Religion tries it in the positive way. Science searches it in the round about way. Science analyses the object. Religion analyses the Subject. Scientific conclusions arrived at by analysing the Object differ variously with each other. But Truth found out by various religions by analysing the subject is always One and the Same.

29th MARCH 1R59

HON. JUSTICE MEETS HIS HOLINESS

Today Swamiji graced the Eye Hospital to get his glasses renewed.

The testing glasses in the 'Trial Case' which have been faithfully and sincerely serving the poor patients had their reward today, by being allowed to adorn the Master's eyes.

After finishing the eye test, Swamiji went to the office. Hon. Justice Sri J.L. Kapoor of the Supreme Court, New Delhi, and his wife who were waiting for Swamiji's Darshan, entered the office.

"Kindly take your seat" requested Swamiji.

Fruits and coffee were served to the guests. "Oji, Bring a set of books" Swamiji ordered.

A heap of books including "Sadhana" was offered to the Justice.

Justice: Thank you Swamiji. I came to know about Your Holiness through Mr. Bhargava.

Swamiji: Justice T. L. Venkatarama Iyer and Justice Sri Chandrasekhara Iyer all used to come here.

Justice: Is it so? They are my best friends.

Glancing at a book, Justice asked:

"We want to know the essence of Vedanta, Swamiji."

"Essence of Vedanta! ......The Individual Soul is identical with the Supreme Soul. In essence we are all Brahman only," Swamiji replied.

Mrs. Kapoor: Are we fortunate to hear a Bhajan from you Swamiji?

Swamiji revealed the essence of Vedanta and the path to attain that Goal, by His short, sweet, soulstirring Kirtan. The guests were deeply moved by Kirtan.

After visiting the Eye Hospital, they did Pranams and took leave of Swamiji.

30th MARCH 1959

ARISE AWAKE

After the night Satsang, Prasad was distributed. Everybody was absorbed in taking the Prasad. Swamiji noticed it.

"How many times have you masticated up till now?" Swamiji himself imitated the action and enquired someone.

"Endless," the reply came.

Swamiji points out how we have wasted our life in eating and drinking alone. Indirectly he reminds us of the Ultimate goal of God-realisation, the higher mission in life one should aim at, besides eating, drinking and sleeping.

"The life is short. Time is fleeting. Arise. Awake. Strive hard and reach the Goal." Such is the ancient call to humanity given by Swamiji, the modern prophet.

SIVA, THE LIBERATED SOUL

Someone has sent Pappad in a vessel in which garlic had been kept once. Even after a long time the garlic smell was there a little. Swamiji remarked about this:

"Even so the Jiwan Muktha has a little Vasana left over and so he has some likes and dislikes."

Here Swamiji reveals himself. "Swamiji also acts, talks, drinks and eats. We also do the same thing. What is the difference then?" Some may think so.

It is something like saying, "Swamiji is having diabetes. I also have it. So there is no differette between us."

If at all we can compare we can very well say that Swamiji rests on Mount and we are at the bottom of Pacific Ocean. So much is the difference between ordinary men and Swamiji.

Swamiji, the liberated Soul appears to be eating, drinking

and acting but not as we do. As much attachment as we have for our actions, so much detachment Swamiji has for his actions.

The electric fan goes on revolving for some time even after the switch is put off. Similar is the case with Swamiji.

SIVA'S RIDDLE–SIVA IS THE ANSWER

Swamiji started back to his kutir. He was in a jovial mood. "Water above the head and water below. Still she is not drenched. Who is she?" Swamiji put a riddle. No body replied. Swamiji himself answered. "A lady with a water pot on her head walks on a river bridge." No No. It is not the lady. I say it is Swamiji. Tears of the devotees, all over the world, who come to him and prostrate before him, flow like water below. His Grace flow like Ganges-water from his eyes, above. So both above and below there is water still he is not drenched because his experience in his own words, is "Nothing exists, Nothing belongs to me, I am neither mind nor body. Immortal Self I am."

Do you agree with my answer; Sir?

COCK LAYS EGGS?

"Where and when the cock lays egg?" Next riddle, Swamiji put.

"Early morning at 5 o' clock in the back-yard of a house cock usually lays eggs," someone replied.

All burst into laughter.

"Cock never lays eggs, my dear Sir!" Swamiji replied with a naughty smile.

Swamiji points out, such is the impossibility to assert the reality of this world. The reality of this world is like cock's egg, barren woman's son and horn of a hare.

THE OMNIPRESENT GOD

It was raining outside. So all had a quick march, back to

Swamiji's Kutir. While entering the Kutir Swamiji did Namaskar to all the devotees by folding his hands behind. Everybody enjoyed the joke.

"Is it right to do Namaskar like that?" someone may think.

Yes. It is correct for Swamiji because he feels "behind is Ram, below is Ram, everywhere is Ram."

Om Tat Sat

31st MARCH 1959

ADVICE TO SUIT ASPIRANT

A retired person whom Swamiji asked to go back to his place, after a few days' stay in the Ashram came this morning and prostrated before Swamiji.

Swamiji: Oji you need not go back. You can stay here and work in the press for few hours daily. Rest of the time you can utilise for your Sadhana."

Aspirant: First you asked me to go back, Swamiji, now you ask me to stay here. I don't know the reason why?

Swamiji: Yes, first I asked you to go back because your mind was not fit enough to stay here but these few days' stay in the Ashram has made you alright. So I ask you to stay here now.

The person agreed and went away.

Swamiji's advice at one time will appear quite contradictory to what he says another time. But it is not so. "Matru Devo Bhava, Pitru Devo Bhava" (Consider mother as God. Consider father as God) may be the advice of Swamiji to an aspirant who comes, leaving his home, in the beginning. But for the same aspirant Swamiji may say after few days that there is no father or mother ("Mata Nasti Pita Nasti") Even though it looks so contradictory, it is only according to the development of the aspirant, Swamiji gives his advice.

GANGA-SAGAR

A group of devotees from Madras came for Swamiji's Darshan. Swamiji enquired one of them.

Swamiji: Is there Ganges in Madras?

Devotee: No Swamiji. But there is sea in Madras. Swamiji:

That is right. This Ganges joins the sea. So the sea also is Ganges. Is it not?

Usually river joins the sea and loses its name as a river. But Ganges is so sacred, it joins the sea and makes the sea purified. Similarly Jnana Ganga of Sivananda flows towards the ocean of humanity and makes it purified.

THE PROPRIETOR AND HIS AGENT

A devotee of Swamiji who is a silk manufacturer was explaining to Swamiji how the silk worn cocoons are killed in thousands for the manufacture of fine Silk. Swamiji's eyes were filled with compassion. He expressed:

"Poor silk worms! What a wonderful sacrifice they do! They sacrifice their very life for men to wear luxurious silk clothes."

Again turning to the devotee Swamiji asked.

Swamiji: Who kills the silk worms?.....The proprietor.

Devotee: No Swamiji. We never kill these worms. Only the machine does it.

Swamiji: Who is the proprietor of the machine?..........!

Swamiji here reveals to us a beautiful subtle lesson.

A man cannot escape thinking, that it is sin only when he himself commits it. To induce others to commit sin, to be a cause for someone to commit sin, is also sin."

FOR SUCCESS IN BUSINESS

Then the topic was about the rich business people. Swamiji remarked that it is not by the quality of the business one becomes rich but it is by God's grace alone one becomes rich. Swamiji said:

"When God wants to make you rich, one becomes a millionaire even by doing a petty business. By selling betel nut, by selling needles, by keeping a coffee hotel so many have become rich. But for God's grace even if you do big business with a capital of lakhs of rupees one gets loss."

Another lesson Swamiji teaches us that one should not feel egoistic of his efficiency in business for merely the efficiency doesn't bring forth success without God's grace.

BE MODERATE

In the night Satsang Sri Darmambal suggested that a 1000W flood lamp should be put up for the dance performance of Sri Mangala, a relative of Sri D.V. Rajan, Calcutta.

Swamiji: Enough. Enough. This light itself is sufficient. You will put 1000W, fuse will go away and we have to lose even this light.

By his remark Swamiji warns the Sadhaka to be always moderate, and not to go to extreme because extreme in any case brings forth loss to the entire thing altogether.
1-4-58.

THE SADHU'S ROLE IN SOCIETY

An invitation to a Bhandara in Swamiji's Kutir with the names of persons who were invited for the same was found pasted in the notice board near the office.

Only later on we were told that it was only to fool everybody as it was "April Fool's Day."

Sri Swami N. came to the Kutir to take leave as he was going to Gujarat to stay with a devotee of Swamiji for sometime.

Swamiji: Oji, don't stay there like a Mahant ordering for milk, fruits and nice food. You have to do some selfless service there. Help him in his hospital work. I will write to him and enquire, alright?

Swamiji N agreed to it and took leave. Then Swamiji generally remarked:

"It is not at all good, Sanyasis go to the village sit idly and order for comforts from the villagers. It shouldn't be so. They must stay in a village, do some service to the people of that locality, elevate them by conducting Kirtans and discourses. Sannyasi's only aim in life is to realise the All-pervading Spirit, which underlies all creation. This can be attained only by serving humanity with Atma Bhav."

THE SANYASIN'S BATH

Pada Pooja was conducted by Sri S.R. Subramania Iyer from Calcutta. During the Pooja Swami Sri Bhagavathananda was sitting there. Swamiji asked him to join in the Pada Pooja.

Swamiji: Bhagavathananda Maharaj, you can also join.

Swami B. No Swamiji. I have not taken my bath yet. Tomorrow I will do.

Swamiji: For you bath is not here in this Gangas. You have to take bath only in the Jnana Ganga (Ganges of Wisdom) Swamiji points out that a Sannyasi need not give so much importance for the external purification, such as taking bath, etc.

A Sanyasi has no Agni (fire) like a householder.

He has the fire of knowledge. He dips daily in the Jnana Ganga and takes bath. He never gives any oblation to any god for he has given himself as oblation in the Vraja Homa.

He should strive hard for his internal purification through which he attains the inner realisation.

2nd APRIL 1959

CURE FOR PHYSICAL AND MENTAL ILLS

Sri Muruga Das, a famous Sankirtanist from Madras who was here yesterday, gave a Sankirtan Recital with his gifted sweet voice. This morning he met Swamiji in his Kutir.

Swamiji: Murugadas Bhagavan, kindly go to the big hospitals in the city and conduct Kirtan and prayer there for the health and long life of the patients. By doing this you can change the atmosphere into a divine one and that will act as a tonic for the quick recovery of the sick people from their illness.

Occasionally go to the Jails and do Kirtan there for the welfare of the prisoners. Hearing of Lord's Name will turn their mind and make them lead a good and honest life hereafter.

Sri Murugadas has agreed to it and took leave of Swamiji.

Swamiji always induces the talent and faculty of any kind, in every man, to blossom forth, and makes use of it in a Divine Way for the welfare of humanity at large. This is how Swamiji, as a single person, has worked so much, which no man can even imagine, for the dissemination of spiritual culture all over the world.

A BOY WITH HEART ON RIGHT SIDE

After the Kirtan Swamiji was about to start back to his Kutir. Just then Sri K.N.P. Nair, House Master, Doon School, Dehra Dun, followed by 18 students came to Swamiji and bowed to him.

Childlike Swamiji was overjoyed to see the children. "Boys, come on! Repeat this." Swamiji started his favourite "Govinda Kirtan" a song of practical spiritual precepts. A faithful following of the teachings contained in the song will mould a student's character and pave the way for his bright future and

85

success in life. Swamiji distributed them "Divine Life for Children" pamphlets, story books as well nice biscuits for them to eat.

Sri Nair introduced a boy to Swamiji, in whom the heart is displaced on the right side of the chest.

Swamiji called for stethoscope and examined the boy.

The boys were very much pleased and took leave of Swamiji after photograph.

Do you all know? Swamiji's Heart also is on the right side. Do you wonder? Yes, his Heart is on the right side. In the words of a Biblical saying:

"A fool's heart is on the left side. But a wise man's heart is on the right side."

3rd APRIL

SAGE OF COSMIC VISION

Sri Peter Schmid a Swiss journalist was staying here in the Ashram for the past two days. This morning he met Swamiji in the office.

Sri Peter: Swamiji, I like one thing here in this Ashram most. That is the simplicity. Here you and your disciples live a very simple life at the same time doing magnificent work. This is something most wonderful. (Turning to the ladies' group) Do these people stay here permanently, Swamiji?

Swamiji: No. No. They are devotees. They come here, stay for a few days and go back . . . . Do you know? Mr. Peter,........one French Journalist came here and stayed for some days. He returned to his country and wrote a book about India in which when describing this Ashram, he has mentioned that "Swamiji was surrounded by his wives in his office."

All burst into laughter.

The office where Swamiji works daily is a small building built several years ago when Swamiji was not having innumerable disciples and devotees as he is having now. It is a usual scene to see the office overcrowded everyday by the thirsting devotees and disciples, who come for Swamiji's Darshan from all over the world. In order to prevent the ladies being crushed in the crowd, Swamiji has permitted them to sit near his chair. This fact had been misunderstood by the materialistic-minded French journalist which made him write such nonsense.

One should clearly understand without the least doubt, that Swamiji has no sex-consciousness in him, as he is the one who is always fixed in the SELF-CONSCIOUSNESS. He sees only the Self in all and not the male or female, young or old, wicked or wise. His is the vision of equality. "If it is the case," some crooked mind may think, "why Swamiji makes the differences at all between men and women." This is due to the improper learning with an incorrect understanding of "EQUALITY."

Equal vision does not consist in making a man stand under a ruined wall and making a donkey to sit in a sofa. Equal vision is a vision of Oneness, a vision of internal Unity underlying the external diversity and difference.

Moreover, it is not only for ladies, Swamiji provides the seat near him. The same facility he gives to the sick and elderly persons also.

Therefore a humble suggestion to westerners who come to India with the intention of learning Yoga and Vedanta, that they should judge things with right understanding and discrimination. Then alone they will be benefited. Otherwise if they see things as the French journalist saw, their condition will be like the one who goes for bath but comes back with mud all over the body.

Sri Peter was wonderstruck when he saw Swamiji's books translated in almost all the languages of the world. He took photograph of all those books. Then he visited the eye hospital, took snaps and gave his appreciation for the simple, neat, selfless service which is done to the sick and the poor. He took leave of Swamiji after lunch.

GOD LIVER OIL

A young lady who appeared very weak came to Swamiji and prostrated before him. She told about her ill-health and asked Swamiji for some remedy.

Swamiji: Take God Liver Oil.......

Devotee: No Swamiji. I have taken plenty of Cod Liver Oil but no use.

Swamiji: Not Cod Liver Oil. I meant GOD LIVER OIL. It

will nourish your mind which in turn will make your body all right.

When allopathy, homeopathy and all other Pathies fail, Swamiji's Divine Nama pathy has cured many persons.

Similarly, this God Liver Oil is a New Nourishing Oil made in Ananda Kutir, manufactured under the guidance of Dr. Sivananada, M.D. Pdm. (Master of Divinity of Paramdham University). If you want it, you need not come here, or write to him, but just sit in your home, pray to him sincerely. From here he treats you with his oil which nourishes both your mind and body then and there. Price is nothing but faith and devotion.

PSEUDO-VEDANTA

A group of four or five ladies from Amritsar came here for Swamiji's Darshan. They met Swamiji in the office.

One of them: Swamiji, we have come from Amritsar. We belong to the Vedantic Ashram. We have studied Vedanta well.

Swamiji: Oh! you have studied Vedanta well....Tell me......Who are you......a Panjabi or Sindhi?

Swamiji here points out that the body idea, i.e., thinking oneself as a male or female, a Hindu or Christian, an Indian or an European, cannot be got over easily by the mere study of Vedanta alone.

One should develop Sadhana Chatushtaya first. He must approach a Guru then and hear the subtle vedantic Truths from him. He must reflect over the Truth again and again. Then intense meditation should be practised for a long time with patience and perseverance. Then alone one rises above the body idea and realise the Essence of Vedanta, that he is the All-pervading Spirit.

Then Swamiji told a very interesting, and instructive story to them.

"A certain man went to a shop, opened the cash-box, took away all the money and walked out. He was caught and brought before the magistrate. When he was asked whether he is guilty he replied, "Your Honour! I am a staunch follower of Vedanta. The Vedanta says 'I am the all. Everything is mine. So according to Vedanta, the shop is mine, the money is mine. Therefore it is not a theft, I did, but faithful following of the Vedantic Truth." The Magistrate was a clever man. He called two strong men and asked them to whip this Vedantic Lion severely till blood oozed out.

Poor Vedantic Lion, instead of roaring, only cried bitterly when he was whipped. The magistrate asked coolly, "Why are you crying now? The same Vedanta says that you are not this body. You are the all-pervading spirit." Thinking there is no escape the thief accepted his mistake. He was convicted for two years.

This instructive story, I hope, will impress some of the so called 'Empty Bullets' who call themselves great Vedantins.

"O man! Develop the spirit of selfless service and sacrifice, Cosmic Love, universal brotherhood, tolerance, forgiveness and equal vision."

This is the precept for practice of Vedanta in daily life proclaimed by Swamiji, the practical Vedantin of the present age.

SECLUSION AMIDST THE CROWD

Swamiji advised a lady who was standing amidst a group of ladies.

"When you are amidst a group you will be dragged unconsciously, for idle talks. So be careful. Do mental Japa. Repeat Lord's Name mentally. By this method you can gain the benefit of seclusion amidst various distractions."

DIVINE LIFE IN A NUTSHELL

An young man came to Swamiji's Kutir this morning. After prostration he asked.

"What is Divine Life, Swamiji?"

Swamiji: Do Japa. Do Kirtan. Practise Pranayam. Serve selflessly. Practise Ahimsa, Satyam, Brahmacharya. That is all. "KRISHNA BHAGWAN KI JAI."

Swamiji has given a very simple, short and practical method. Alright. But what is that "Krishna Bhagawan Ki Jai"? What does He mean by that. What does He emphasise by that?

"O Man! You need not break your head by reading variety of books by different authors with their different interpretations if at all you want to lead a Divine Life. They are written, not to make a man evolve, but to show only their erudition. After studying all those books one gets, not a correct conception of Divine Life, but only confusion of the mind, The essence of all the scriptures in the world is contained in these five words, "SERVE LOVE PURIFY MEDITATE REALIZE."

Therefore start here and now; Strive hard; reach the Goal, and become Divine."

Do you understand now.......why Swamiji emphasised "That is all. Krishna Bhagawan Ki Jai."

GUIDING LIGHT

Swamiji's reply to his devotees is a soothing balm of consolation, a perpetual source of inspiration and a guiding light for illumination, not only for the devotee concerned but to the whole world at large.

Here is a specimen of a letter, He wrote today to a devotee in Lucknow.

Glorious Immortal Atman!

Thy kind letter. Weakness comes when one forgets his essential, divine nature. Kindly increase your period of Japa and meditation. Be bold. Be courageous. Be calm. Be positive always. Look within. Gaze within. Plunge within. Tap the source. Within is the magazine of power, wisdom and strength. Thou art Omnipotent, Omniscient. Behold the Atman everywhere.

Detachment, aspiration, identification with the Immortal Atman, meditation are the ingredients of success, victory, peace, joy and bliss.

Draw inspiration and strength from within through meditation.

Let not a little disharmony and opposition upset you. You are invulnerable. Stand on the rock of Atmic strength.

March forward. O Adhyatmic hero, with strong determination, strong will, resoluteness and perseverance. Look not back.

Aim at perfection. Fight life's battle bravely. Strengthen your resolution. Claim the peak of perfection. Rest in thy Satchidananda Swaroop. Examine. Analyse. Know. All problems will be solved. I am conducting prayer for your health, peace, strength and illumination.

May Lord bless you. Om Tat Sat. Thy own Atman.

One can feel within, the integral transformation which takes place while going through this letter. They are not merely a garland of words. The boundless compassion, he feels in his heart, flows through his hands to the heart of the devotee who is in distress.

Swamiji was remarking while giving this letter for dispatching "Vedanta alone can console a person who is in despondency. Vedanta is the magnanimous philosophy which helps the aspirants to eradicate fear, sorrow, grief, delusion and raises him to the sublime heights of Brahmanhood."

7th APRIL 1959

LEAD A SIMPLE LIFE

A devotee from Japan has sent a photo Album and a fancy handmade fan. It was shown to Swamiji. Swamiji started fanning himself, and humorously remarked,

"Oh! wonderful fan…..! it is giving plenty of breeze?"

The fan was made just for fancy. It will serve only to increase the artificiality of a fashionable lady, nothing more and nothing less. By his remark Swamiji points out that many of the fancy articles which are used by the modern materialistic men these days, only help to empty his purse to satisfy his vain vanity and are not at all useful in any way whatsoever.

Swamiji advises the modern man to lead a modest, simple and contented life which alone makes a man really noble and gentle.

WHERE TO SETTLE DOWN

An old person entered the office. He approached Swamiji and introduced himself.

Old person: Swamiji, I am retired from my service now. I am Radiologist. I want to settle somewhere…….

Swamiji: Settle in your heart.

Swamiji reveals that real settlement is not to settle in a fine bungalow on a river bank with a fixed-deposit in a bank and spend the last days after retirement wasting your time without any useful purpose.

Real settlement is to settle in one's own heart where alone one rests peacefully for ever and enjoys the everlasting happiness.

Finally the retired doctor decided to settle in the Ashram

after sometime. Then it is certain, he will settle in his heart also by the able guidance of Swamiji who is already settled in his heart and rests there happily.

GIVE UP VANITY

After the night Satsang Swamiji was just starting back to his Kutir. Sri John Banman, an aspirant from Vancouver was standing in front of Swamiji.

"Oh! is it John Banman? I couldn't recognise you. What is the matter?" Swamiji enquired.

Someone said that he has removed his moustache, that is the reason why he couldn't be recognised easily.

"That is it......Then you have done Ego-dectomy, I think." Swamiji remarked.

Swamiji points out that even the moustache can make a man feel egoistic. Shaving of moustache means cutting of the egoism a little. So many things in man increase his egoism. Moustache is one among them. "The more moustache the more egoism. The more egoism is the direct road to the hell." So says Swamiji in his "Wisdom in Humour."

9th APRIL 1959

SIVANANDA REGALIA

Swamiji emerged from his Kutir this morning, a bit early and went straight to visit Regalia.

Regalia is an interesting place to be seen by everyone who comes to the Ashram, where a collection of Swamiji's personal articles which were used by Him, are kept arranged nicely. Each one, if you go and ask them, will narrate you an interesting story of Swami Sivananda, about his inspiring life, his divine mission, his spiritual achievement and about his unparalleled greatness.

The personal articles of Swamiji which were used by him long ago, were smiling to see their Master after a long time.

The various presents which are kept there, sent by the devotees from various parts of the world, proclaim his name and fame, spread all over the globe.

A full set of over 300 books written by Swamiji and more than 150 books written on Swamiji, by eminent men of all fields of East and West proclaims the oceanic depth of his spiritual knowledge. They are the open proofs of the impressive expression of his inner experience.

The small pamphlet published 30 years ago and the bumper volume "Sadhana", published a few months back openly proclaim the 30 years of untiring selfless service of The Divine Life Society in disseminating the spiritual knowledge to humanity at large.

The books which are translated in different foreign languages convey to us, how the message of Swamiji has reached far and wide even to the remotest corner of S. America.

In fact, every item in the Regalia is imparting the STORY OF SWAMI SIVANANDA.

SPEND MORE TIME ON INNER CULTURE

Swamiji came out of the Regalia. He was proceeding to the Office. A Vaishnava devotee from South India with the Vaishnavite Marks all over his body, approached Swamiji and bowed to him.

"How long did you take to decorate yourself with these marks?" Swamiji enquired him.

"About half an hour," he replied. "Half an hour!" Swamiji exclaimed.

The expression on Swamiji's face clearly expresses, "O Man! Don't waste your time and energy in decorating yourself with these external marks to show that you are Vishnu Bhakta or Siva Bhakta. God never considers these external shows. He expects the inner purity. A real Vaishnava or Saiva is the one who is pure in his heart, who loves all, who serves all, who sees the same Lord in all beings, who has controlled lust, greed and anger and not the one who puts merely the external marks on his body".

MANAHKALPITAM JAGAT

Some devotee brought 'Jilebi a kind of sweetmeat to Swamiji. Swamiji tasted a little and asked for more as it was prepared very nicely. Somebody interrupted, "Swamiji, kindly don't take it, it is not prepared in ghee. So it is not a good one."

Swamiji said, "It is not the ghee which makes the Jilebi tasty, but it is one's own liking for it which makes it tasty."

Swamiji points out that the objects of the world have no pleasure-giving nature in themselves. But it is man's liking and craving for the objects which makes them pleasurable. For example, if you say that milk is tasty, it should give the same taste to one and all, at all times. But one person tastes the milk like anything, the same milk, the other vomits at once. This clearly proves, that there is no 'good or bad' in the objects but it is man who makes them so.

10th APRIL 1959

"Sri Swami Ranganathanandaji......" Swamiji called him during the night Satsang for lecture.

"He is bitten by scorpion, Swamiji" someone replied.

"Summer season has started. We must take some precautions to avoid scorpion bites," somebody remarked.

"Nothing will do. If at all you are to be bitten by scorpion it will happen on any account. All your precautions are of no use," Swamiji replied.

Swamiji explains by his remark that man cannot simply escape the suffering, he has to undergo through ADHIBHAUTIKA (the pain one undergoes due to the earthquakes, thunders, floods, snake and scorpion bites, etc., are called the pains of Adhibhautika) by taking some precautions. It is the natural Law, every Jiva has to undergo the three kinds of sufferings Adhyatmika, Adhidaivika and Adhibhautika. Therefore one has to endure them patiently because they are only passing phenomena. Enduring them one should strive hard and march forward towards the Ultimate Goal.

11th APRIL 1959

Swamiji was enquiring about the recent marriage of a devotee's daughter. She was describing how unknown persons also offered the bride with costly presents during the marriage.

"Oh, it is because of the high position and rank of the bridegroom's father. The presents were given just due to the fear of the position and with selfish motive, and not because of love or anything. If the position goes, the so-called love and respect also will go along with it. That is the nature of the world," Swamiji replied.

Swamiji reveals the inner secret behind the so-called love and affection and respect of the worldly people. So far there is money, property, position and rank with you, all persons will crowd around you in the name of relatives, friends and well-wishers. The moment your position and property goes even a crow will not fly near you. Such is the nature of the world. Therefore O Men ! Detach yourself from the attachment of this fleeting world and attach yourself with Lord who alone is your real friend, guide and well-wisher.

Swamiji was proceeding to the office.

"We are in very bad need of latrines with flush-out system in the Ashram," someone passed a remark.

"More than that we need flush-out system for our brain very badly," Swamiji replied.

Swamiji points out that evil Vasanas (tendencies) which are collected in innumerable births are gathered in man's brain and stand stagnated. The smell of lust, greed, hatred, jealousy are spread from him all over. Therefore he should be thoroughly cleansed with flush-out system of service, sacrifice, Satsang, study, Japa and meditation.

99

12th APRIL 1959

A REMEDY FOR EVERYTHING

Dr. Sri D. K. Viswanathan, Malarial Adviser, World Health Organization, who is a staunch devotee of Swamiji, came here for Darshan with his wife and son, and to have blessings of Swamiji before his leaving for Switzerland on service.

During the breakfast Swamiji gave him 'Adai' (a south Indian Preparation).

"Is it not nice," Swamiji enquired.

"Yes, Swamiji, very nice," Sri Viswanathan replied,

"If it is known that Swamiji likes it, I would have prepared the flower paste for the Adai at Delhi itself and brought it here for Swamiji," Mrs Viswanathan said.

"It is not possible. It will be spoiled then" Swamiji remarked.

"No Swamiji......It won't......if you bring it in a flask," Mrs Viswanathan replied.

"That is wonderful—See! for everything man has got a remedy. That is the beauty of God's creation." Swamiji remarked.

Swamiji points out that negative forces do exist in this world. But there exist remedies also for everything side by side. Negative forces are created in this world just in order to make man's intellect positively developed to overcome the negative. It is only the havoc done by the Malaria mosquitoes that has given rise to the invention of Comoquaine the anti-malarial tablets. It is only the sufferings of birth and death, disease and old age that has given rise to 'Buddhas and Sankaras', 'Christs and Nanaks' who have founded out different religions, philosophies, and methods and given men the impetus to strive to overcome those evils, and enjoy the everlasting bliss and peace eternal.

NATURE OF THE WORLD

"In spite of having all the comforts and facilities in life. I don't know why my wife says that she has no peace of mind and she goes on worrying for nothing, Swamiji alone has to make her alright. I have tried my level best......I couldn't........Only Swamiji's grace can do......." A devotee pleaded to Swamiji.

"That is the nature of this world. That is Maya's powerful play. She has created such a mind with some peculiar constituents and does all this mischief," Swamiji remarked.

The devotee approached Swamiji with a prayerful attitude and prostrated before Swamiji.

"Bless me with discrimination, Swamiji," she prayed.

Swamiji pacified her and conducted prayer and Mrityunjaya Japa. Then she felt relieved.

HOW TO GET SOUND SLEEP?

Sri Rishiram, son of Dr. Sri Het Ram Agarwal of Amritsar prostrated before Swamiji.

"Swamiji, can you please tell me some remedy for my sleeplessness. I couldn't bear the suffering," Sri Rishi Ram requested Swamiji.

"Oji, I will tell you a new medicine. Sit on your bed. Repeat this Mantra. Yaa Devee Sarvabhuteshu Nidrarupena Samsthita, Namasthasyai Namasthasyai Namasthasyai Namo Namah."

Remember the following names and pray to the sound sleepers.

"As Asthik, Agasthya, Kapila, Modhaser and Muchukunda." Mother Parasakthi will bestow sound sleep.

PRAYER

"How can you explain the efficacy of prayer in a scientific manner, Swamiji?" A person with a little of rational temperament approached Swamiji and asked this question.

"By prayer a connection is established between the devotee and God. A channel is made for the flow of divine Grace and blessing from God to the devotee," Swamiji replied.

His was a question and not a request. That shows a little bit of ego in the person. So Swamiji's grace in the form of his answer did not flow in full floods. If the person would have approached Swamiji with a prayerful attitude for the clarification of his doubt about prayer, perhaps, Swamiji would have given him the following reply in a more scientific manner.,

"Prayer is a surrendering attitude of a person, where he realises his individual weakness, accepts and expects the Divine Force to work out in Its own way. That which obstructs the Divine Grace to flow, is the individual ego in man. Therefore the moment the individual ego is surrendered to the Divine by prayer, a connection is automatically established between God and devotee through which a channel is made for the flow of Divine Grace and blessing."

14th APRIL 1959

TO BE FAR IS TO BE NEAR

Swamiji made his appearance today at 9 a.m. The quiet simplicity of his plain clothes of exquisite neatness, made his personality shine with greater lustre. The golden colour of his body was glittering through the thin upper cloth he was wearing.

Soon after Swamiji seated himself in the chair, Sri Venkatesanandaji handed over a cheque, sent by a devotee who is at present in London. He has requested for a Pada Pooja to be done in his name on Rama Navami day.

"The more one is away, the more devotion is developed," Swamiji remarked.

Swamiji imparts a lesson to those who stay near him. We fail to recognise always the greatness of a saint when we are close to him. Only when we are away from him, we miss him badly.

It is a well-known fact that those who live near the temples go late for the worship.

Even God withdraws His Presence from the devotee sometimes, in order to make the devotee feel His separation which in turn increases his devotion.

To go far away from a saint physically is to come closer to him mentally.

Swamiji's warm welcome will be for those who come closer to him in their hearts.

PATNI SEVA

Just then a middle aged person came and prostrated before Swamiji.

"I was suffering with an ailment for a long time Swamiji. As per your advice I repeated the Maha Mrityunjaya Mantra. Now I am perfectly alright, I have come for your Darshan with my wife." He expressed his gratitude to Swamiji.

Turning to the wife, Swamiji said "Oji do Pati Seva."

Looking at the husband, "Oji you have to do Patni Seva."

It is not a mere joke, what Swamiji said. It is a practical philosophy of 'Home Affairs' following which you can make your own house into heaven there itself.

It is a fact. Wife is not merely a slave in the hands of the husband, or a product purchased in the marriage market for the enjoyment of your desires.

She is your life's partner who shares your pain and pleasure, so to say, she is half of your personality.

Therefore Swamiji stresses that it is not that wife alone has to serve the husband and please him in all possible ways. There should be a mutual sharing of service between each other. Each one must be a friend, guide and beloved to the other.

Such couples make the house, a heaven and enjoy the life happily.

EXAMINER IS EXAMINED

Sri Ramachandran from Penang, a devotee of Swamiji, took the activities of the Eye Hospital in movie films this morning. Swamiji graced the hospital with his holy presence.

When the shooting was going on, at a particular time, Dr. Sivananda Hridayananda was sitting by the side of Swamiji. To the surprise of the doctor, Swamiji examined her eyes.

It was a wonderful scene. Dr. Hridayananda, the eye-surgeon who diagnoses the cataract of all the eyes, was examined by the Surgeon Sivananda who alone can diagnose, and remove the cataract of the mind of all men, and give the vision of intuition, Surgeon Sivananda prescribes the glasses of wisdom and devotion, fixed in the frame of selfless service to have the vision of intuition.

OBEY THE RULES

Then Swamiji proceeded to the office.

A young man came to the office and introduced himself as the relieving station master of Madurai.

He prostrated before Swamiji.

"Swamiji, I have been deputed by the Government of India to work as a Station Master in Iraq," the young man informed Swamiji.

"Very glad. When are you going there?" Swamiji enquired.

"I don't know the full details of it, Swamiji. The day I started for Rishikesh, I got the information that I must get prepared for a test, finishing which I will be posted in Iraq. That is all I know. I don't want to leave the trip to Rishikesh. So I left everything as it is and came here."

"You have done a wrong thing. You should not violate the rules on any account. You should have waited there till further orders." Swamiji corrected him.

Swamiji's idea is that one should not violate the rules and regulations, Law and order of a higher authority when you are working under him, on any account and on any excuse.

"Swamiji, I take leave, kindly bless me" the young person prayed to Swamiji.

Looking at him Swamiji smilingly said.

"Oji try to get a transfer to Brahmapuri or Niralambapuri. That alone is your real home."

Swamiji points out that we are caught up in a foreign land where we have no independence of our own leading a life of slavery entirely depending upon the foreigners. This world is a foreign land. The mind and the senses are the foreigners. Our original home is Brahmapuri, the place of everlasting peace and bliss. To reach the home first of all we must develop discrimination to realise that we are caught up in a foreign Land. This discrimination gives rise to dispassion to the life in the foreign land and induces aspiration to reach our original home. Then we search for a guide who can take us to our homeland. Finally, with his guidance we reach our original abode.

But, O man, why to struggle so much for this? Just come to Sivanandanagar and stay here with Swamiji. He will take care of you. He will give you discrimination, dispassion, aspiration and guide you and take you to your original home.

Therefore leave off your worry. Come to Swamiji. Get the key from him. Open the door, enter in, and rest peacefully and happily.

WILL YOU......?!!

During a conversation with Sri Rishi Ram, Swamiji remarked, "Except God, man learns everything."

By learning everything else, you forget God. But to learn God, you have to unlearn everything else. Moreover God is the fruit of all learning as well as the origin. Therefore learn God first, all other learning will be added unto it.

15th April 1959

ERUDITION VS. DEVOTION

Today morning Sri Murali, daughter of Sri Sivananda Nilakantan, Calcutta came to Swamiji's Kutir. She wanted to take Swamiji's Pada Tirtha (holy water of the sacred Feet) with her, Swami Venkatesananda, Satyagnanam and Shantananda started chanting Mantras while she was washing Swamiji's sacred Feet.

Swami Shantananda was chanting the Mantra with half opened lips for he does not know that particular Mantra well. Noticing this Swamiji told a story.

"A certain man, while doing Pooja to Lord Shiva was going on chanting "NAMACHAMA" "NAMACHAMA" "NAMACHAMA." Somewhere he has heard, pandits chanting 'Rudram' and 'Chamakam' in some Siva Temples. He has caught only these two words "Nama—Chama" which are often repeated during the chanting of Rudram and Chamakam. Even though he was chanting with a wrong pronunciation, he was doing the worship with full Bhava and faith. While he was doing thus a Pandit came there and told him that it was wrong to chant like that and Lord Siva would not accept his Pooja.

On the same night Lord Siva appeared and told the Pandit in his dream that He was very much pleased with the person's worship even with his wrong pronunciation as he was doing the Pooja with sincerity and devotion.

Swamiji imparts a lesson to all the Pandits who chant Mantras without any Bhava or devotion in them, Lord is pleased not with the gramaphone-like repetition of His Names, but the intensity of devotion with which you repeat His Names.

Develop devotion with internal Bhava (Feeling) which

107

moulds your Swabhava (nature) to realise the state of Mahabhava.

SHAVEN-HEADED IN THIRUPATHI?

Swamiji was in the office. A young man from Ceylon came and prostrated before him,

Swamiji enquired about him and gave him some books.

"Swamiji, one of my friends came here last year. You gave him some medicine. He wants it again now," the young man said.

"What medicine it is?, Swamiji enquired.

"I don't know Swamiji. You are preparing it here. That is what my friend told." the person replied.

Swamiji remarked, "It is something like searching for a Shaven-head man in Tirupathi. No body can identify a person if you say he is a Swami in Rishikesh. Rishikesh is full of Swamis and Sannyasis."

All burst into laughter.

Then Swamiji himself guessed that it is Chyavanaprash he has asked and gave him a tin.

The person was pleased and took leave of Swamiji.

GIFTED LIFE

"Life is a gift or loan," Swamiji enquired Venkatesanandaji.

"We can say both Swamiji," he replied.

Swamiji clarified it. "Life becomes a gift when one utilises this rarely gifted human body in achieving immortality in this very life itself.

Life becomes loan for those who waste it in eating, drinking and sleeping."

In other sense this life is a gifted-loan given by God. You invest it as a capital to gain the profit of everlasting happiness. Surrendering the fruits of all your actions to Lord is the 'Interest' you pay for the loan. The entire loan is repaid when you surrender your individual personality itself.

Then you become a free capitalist of the Eternal Wealth of Atma.

17th APRIL 1959

WHO IS AN ARYAN?

Swamiji was engaged in his usual routine work in the office. A devotee brought some chocholates. Dr. Hridayananda was sitting by the side of Swamiji. Shantanandaji was distributing the Prasad.

"Shantananda! If you give me those chocholates, I will give you this," joked Swami Hridayananda, offering him a peace of cocoanut.

"Yes Mataji, but you have to give me the cocoaut first" replied Shantananda offering her two chocolates.

Swamiji was listening to this conversation.

"Oji, Don't do this exchange business. Return the cocoanut. Give her chocholates, plenty of them. Be generous. To exchange is 'Un-Aryan' and turning to a devotee, "One who is noble and truthful and generous is an Aryan."

Swamiji beautifully clarifies the word "ARYAN" for which there have been so much controversies among the historians. The word 'Aryan' often quoted in our Epic and Puranas does not indicate a particular race or creed. According to Swamiji Aryan is one who is noble and truthful, pure and straightforward in heart.

SATIETY

Just then Swami Raghunath brought some fried Pappad said to have been sent by a devotee from Hapur. They were distributed.

"O this is not nice. Some sort of smell comes in this" someone remarked about the Pappad.

"Yes, yes. How can it be? Just now you had Halva and

Sweetmeats. When one is hungry, anything will be tasty. Starved-cow will simply swallow anything you keep in front of it," Swamiji replied with naughty smile.

Swamiji points out a grand truth which we are not aware of even though it happens in our daily life.

When your stomach is full, even the tastiest thing you cannot enjoy. A sweetest thing becomes sweeter when you take twice. Third time it will become only sweet and the subsequent times if you are compelled to take it, you vomit it. This clearly proves the objects of this world give only temporary and not everlasting enjoyment.

A saint has no inclination to enjoy the worldly pleasures as he is ever full in his heart.

Therefore attain that fullness and enjoy the happiness everlasting.

SWAMIJI....THE REMEMBRANCE

In the night Satsang Swami Chidanandaji was giving a discourse on 'Points to Remember,' during which he kept a point pending to be explained later. But in the end he had altogether forgotten about it. When he was about to finish his discourse Swamiji reminded him.

"Chidananda Swamiji, Kindly remember the point you said you will explain later."

All burst into laughter.

Instead of trying to remember so many "points to remember," it is better if we remember Swamiji, the remembrancer.

Swamiji's Name itself is a remembrancer which reminds us the greatness of Mother India who gave birth to so many saints and savants in the past and present.

Swamiji's personality is a remembrancer which reminds us to recognise him as people's preceptor.

Swamiji's sparkling eyes are a remembrancer which reminds us of the beauty and grandeur of Atma.

Swamiji's life is a remembrancer which reminds us Lord Krishna's guarantee in Bhagavad Gita (Sambhavami Yuge Yuge) Swamiji's voice is a remembrancer which reminds us of the glory of the celestial sound 'Omkara'.

Swamiji's heart is a remembrancer which reminds us the boundless compassion of the Almighty.

Swamiji's look is a remembrancer which reminds us the infinite Grace of God.

Swamiji's Ashram is a remembrancer which reminds us the necessity of integral development in our personality.

Swamiji's sacred feet are a remembrancer which reminds us the celestial Vimana which takes one to heaven.

Swamiji's hands are a remembrancer which reminds us of the giving heart of Annapoorna Devi. "My God.....!! I am unable to remember everything of this remembrancer for they are endless!"

20th APRIL 1959

SIVANANDA LEELA

It being a cloudy day, visitors were few in number. At about 9.30 we had Swamiji's Darshan, in his Kutir. Sri Sister Daya of Self-realisation Fellowship was expected with her party, Swamiji made his usual kind enquiries about arrangements made for her reception. Turning to Sri Venkatesanandaji Swamiji asked:

"How many of you will always be able to see Lord Narayana in the form of poor beggers?

"It is very difficult to keep that attitude always, Swamiji." replied Sri Venkatesanandaji.

Then Swamiji himself remarked.

"It is all Lord's Leela. He alone takes the part of a beggar and suffers. It is something like a king acting the part of poor person and undergoing all sufferings. They are merely a play for him. The whole creation, all the beings, their pleasures and pain, sorrows and sufferings of this world are nothing but Lord's Leela."

Turning to Sri Venkatesanandaji Swamiji again enquired:

"In that case, how do you account the Law of Karma?"

Sri Venkatesanandaji kept quiet.

Swamiji himself answered.

"In the long process of evolution, in the initial stages, when he is not ripe enough, man follows the Law of Karma. He believes in God who is dispenser of fruits of his actions according to the merit. Therefore he tries to do good actions which in turn give him better chances, circumstances and environments in life, for his further evolution.

"By this he gains purification of heart. For him, the Law of

Karma loses its value now. He feels that he is an instrument in the hands of the Lord. With this attitude when he does his actions, he gets release from the action-reaction process.

"In course of time, as he gets more purification, he transcends even this attitude of thinking that he is an instrument. Now he realises the identity with the Lord and feels His Presence within and without, always. The Karma Theory has no meaning for Him.

"Where does the question arise for the one who feels both the actor and action, as God.

"Who acts, for whom, with what?" is his experience."

Swamiji finished and looked at us all.

"Swamiji was describing Lord's Leela. But What about Himself" Sri Hridayananda whispered to me.

Yes. Swamiji put the question and he himself gave the answer.

Swamiji himself is the 'Question' and the questioner as well...

Swamiji himself is the 'answer' and the answerer as well.

Do you wonder what it is?!

Yes. This is called "SIVANANDA LEELA."

MIRACLE OF SIVANANDA

Sri Venu, a young boy, son of Sri K.C. Gupta, a patron of Divine Life Society, is spending his holidays in the holy company of Swamiji, here in Sivanandanagar. He came and prostrated before Swamiji and straightaway asked: "Swamiji have you seen God."

"Have you seen God," Swamiji asked.

"Swamiji, I have seen God!"

"What!" exclaimed Swamiji. "Where is He then?" "He is sitting in front of me," pointing to Swamiji he politely said.

"Can God wear spectacles?" Swamiji joked him. "Why not?" came the bold reply.

It is not merely an intelligent reply he gave. The conviction he has, was flowing through his eyes. It is a doubtless assertion.

Is it not a wonder for a young boy of 'teens', brought up in a modern society who knows nothing more than cinema show, icecream and cricket match which are common to most of the youngsters of the present day, to have such a conviction to recognise Swamiji as God!

How has his three days' stay with Swamiji, transformed and moulded him to such an extent?!

Now he learns Yoga Asans, Pranayam and also delivers short discourses in the Night Satsang.

Here is a humble suggestion to all the parents that they should send their children to Ananda Kutir during their holidays. They are sure to get a spiritual moulding here in the company of Children's Sivananda, which they lack in the modern education.

"Send the bronze here to Sivanandanagar. GOLD........!!! you will get back . . sure."

This is the MIRACLE OF SIVANANDA'S TOUCH.

SISTER DAYA WITH SIVANANDA

Swamiji was in the office. Routine work was going on.

"Swamiji, they have come" someone informed of the arrival of Sister Daya and her party.

"Oji bring some chairs. Arrange for coffee and biscuits. Bring four sets of books." One by one Swamiji was ordering.

Then Swamiji introduced all the western disciples to the guests.

"He is from California."

"She is from Puerto Rico."

"He is from Trinidad."

"He is from Ghana, Africa."

He is from Israel." "He is from Vancouver." "She is from Hongkong." "He is from Australia."

When Swamiji was introducing thus, the guests were wonderstruck.

They are having a tour around the world. They go from country to country. Here the whole world is moving around Swamiji.

Then the guests were entertained with Bhajan, music, Veena-recital, etc.

Swamiji took them round the Ashram, showed them the General Hospital, Eye Hospital, Research Institute, Regalia, Pharmacy etc.

They were thrilled and expressed their whole hearted appreciation for Swamiji's magnanimous work.

Their car was filled with Swamiji books, Ayurvedic products fruits and sweets, etc.

Swamiji bid them farewell with his OM chanting. With the lovely memory of Ananda Kutir, they took leave.

23rd APRIL 1959

SIVANANDA AMRITAM

Today morning Swami Hridayananda recorded Swamiji's 'Amrita Gita' in the tape-recorder.

The wisdom nectar which once flowed through Swamiji's pen in the book form few years ago, once again was flowing to-day through his mouth.

The recording was in the form of questions and answers.

Sri Swami Hridayananda, the Moksha Priya, (one who yearns for liberation) asked the questions and Swamiji, the liberated one, cleared the doubts of the aspirant with his answers.

After finishing the recording Swamiji came to the office.

Kirtan and prayer was over. Swamiji's eyes fell upon Sri Venu who was sitting in front of him.

"O, Venu has become thin within two days after coming here," Swamiji observed.

"No Swamiji, I am mentally strong," came the smart reply from the young boy.

Those who come to Sivanandanagar get sumptuous spiritual food for the mind.

Sumptuous food to the body, only makes it fat and not strong.

But spiritual food which Swamiji gives you to your mind makes it not fat but strong.

MEANING OF GURU BHAKTI

A disciple of Maa Ananda Mayee entered and bowed to Swamiji. Swamiji called her near to give her some prasad. Before giving the Prasad he joked.

"Are you Ananda Mayee Cheli or Sivananda Cheli?"

117

"Ananda Mayee Cheli, Swamiji," hesitatingly she said.

"Not Sivananda Cheli?" Swamiji asked her with a smile.

"Always one is good, is it not, Swamiji" she again replied.

"That is good. Then be Ananda Mayee Cheli and Sivananda Premi. (Laughter)

Swamiji gives a beautiful hint for the aspirant, who in most of the cases, wrongly understand the devotion to their particular Guru.

It is true that one should have only one Guru. This does not mean he should not even have love or reverence to other saints.

The observance of All Saints Day in the Ashram, is a practical demonstration of the fact that Swamiji's disciples adore him as their Guru, and at the same time have respect and reverence to other saints also.

BLESSING IN DISGUISE

Swamiji turned to Sri Atmaram who recently went back to his home and returned after a short stay.

"How did you enjoy the trip, Atmaramji?" Swamiji asked.

"More than anything else, I have learnt a lesson Swamiji. Those friends who had gained so many obligations when I was in service never even talked to me, just because I have nothing now to oblige them in any way. Even my son was angry with me and didn't even talk to me."

"Have you understood the world now?" Swamiji asked.

"Yes Swamiji."

"Vairagya should have increased now," Swamiji observed.

"Yes Swamiji, definitely."

"Are you ready for Sannyas now?" Swamiji enquired with a smile.

"Not yet Swamiji," Atmaramji hesitated.

God's grace works in so many ways to increase the Vairagya of the sincere and devoted aspirants. Suppose Atmaramji would have had a warm reception there in his home, probably his Vairagya would have had a shake. He would have hesitated even to come back to Rishikesh. It is because God's Grace was there on him, it made the relatives to act in such a way, he got disgust and returned back soon with an increase of dispassion.

24th APRIL 1959

POINTS TO REMEMBER

Today also, the tape recording was continued. Swamiji gave Darshan to his devotees at 10 a.m.

Swami Venkatesanandaji entered.

"Venkatesa Bhagawan, do you remember there is a Pada Pooja and Bhandara on 27th?" Swamiji asked.

"Yes Swamiji, I know."

Swamiji turned to Sri Amaranandaji.

"Oji, Do you remember, two days before I gave you an article for typing?"

"Yes Swamiji, it is the article 'Points to Remember. Here it is Swamiji. I have typed." Amaranandaji gave back the article.

"Atmaramji, remember these points well" Swamiji addressed Atmaramji.

"Remember: Eternal vigilance is the price of salvation.

Remember: earnestness, tenacity, seriousness and application are necessary for the aspirants to advance in the spiritual path.

Remember: always God and the purpose of life.

Remember: Time is very precious. Time once wasted is lost for ever.

Remember: without control of senses and mind, without self-restraint and discipline, one cannot attain God-realisation.

SWAMIJI, THE SUPERMAN

During the night Satsang an old man requested Swamiji that he should be given a chance to sing before Swamiji.

Immediately Swamiji gave him the first chance and asked him to go to the dais.

Practically the person did not know any music. The way in which he sang was something unbearable. Everyone in the Satsang felt bored and slowly they started laughing and joking.

Swamiji was the only person who was sitting there calmly and quietly.

Swamiji allowed him to sing for 10 minutes and then requested him not to exert much and asked him to come down.

This incident sheds light on Swamiji by which we are able to realise the inner reality of his outer personality.

"He who is everywhere without attachment, on meeting anything good or bad, who neither rejoices nor hates, is the one of steadfast wisdom."

Swamiji is the visible manifestation of the above description of a 'Sthithaprajna' as the Lord reveals in His Gita.

When there is a nice programme in the satsangh, where a great songster shows his talent in music, when everybody enjoys, appreciates and claps hands, you can see Swamiji sitting in a calm and serene mood, simply witnessing the function.

Only in the end Swamiji will appreciate the person, saying that he was thrilled by his music. It is not that, that Swamiji was really thrilled. But it is only an encouraging word to make the person concerned feel happy.

Moreover it is only Swamiji, who alone has the courage to ask an ordinary person, who knows not much in music, to sing immediately after a grand recital of a great musician and that also in his very presence.

The reason is this, that Swamiji is ever steadfast in his wisdom. He is in a state, beyond the pairs of opposites. He neither likes anything that is good nor dislikes anything that is bad. His is a state which passeth both good and bad, likes and dislikes, pleasure and, pain.

He is a 'Gunatita' in the words of Bhagavad Gita.

Hundreds of incidents one can witness everyday in Swamiji's Day to Day life. He is a running commentary on the age-old scriptures.

Every action of his interprets in an unique way, the Lord's description of 'Super-Man' in the Bhagavad Gita.

Every word which proceeds from his mouth is a word of wisdom that echo from his Heart and enlighten the whole world.

Prepare your heart, make it a 'well-receiving-set', avoid all sorts of disturbances, so that those words will reecho in you and make you immortal.

27th APRIL 1959

MANTRA DIKSHA

This morning as soon as the Kutir was thrown open Sri M.R. Naidu, a devoted South African aspirant came to Swamiji with his wife. After prostration he prayed for Mantra Diksha.

"Oji, bring Japa Mala, …Om Sri Ramaya Namah…Om Sri Ramaya Namah…Om Sri Ramaya Namah…..Oji, do maximum 200 Malas and minimum 5 Malas of Japa daily. Study Ramayana. Meditate on the Form of Lord Rama. Fast on Ekadasi or once in a month. Om Tat Sat."

Mantra Diksha was over.

"Have you taken any Mantra" Swamiji turned and asked Srimati Bapamma, wife of Sri M.R. Naidu.

"Last year I had initiation from you Swamiji but it was by post."

"Then….come on….take it now in person" Swamiji initiated her also.

Then Swamiji narrated an interesting story.

AN INTERESTING STORY

"Once a person had been to Rameswaram on pilgrimage. He wanted to have sea bath. He went to the sea and kept his vessel on the seashore, made a Linga in the sand by the side of the vessel, so that he could again find it out easily after bath. When he went for bath, another man was watching this. He also did the same thing, prepared a Linga and went for bath. A third person came and did the same thing, thinking it was the custom to do like that. Like this, by the time he returned after the bath, to his surprise he saw hundreds of Lingas and he couldn't make out the exact place where he kept the vessel.

123

Man, due to his attachment, takes so much of precautions to save his worldly possessions, but only suffers in the end.

Blind following leads us nowhere.

"Detach and discriminate" are the two morals, the above story gives us.

IS THIS SELF-CONTROL!

Then Swamiji proceeded to the office. An old man, in whom seeing and hearing are slowly departing, who stays in Rishikesh town, came for Swamiji's Darshan.

Swamiji greeted him and offered him a chair.

"How are you—getting on well?" Swamiji kindly enquired.

"Quite well, Swamiji. Nowadays I have no inclination for anything Swamiji. I never go out of my Kutir. Have some little food, study Ramayana and keep quiet. . This is my daily routine. No craving. No attachment. Nothing." The old man replied in tone as if he has achieved the highest.

Then Swamiji gave him some Prasad and fruits. He took leave of Swamiji.

"No sight. No hearing. Body is not in a condition to move out of his Kutir. Now he says he has no attachment or craving. Wonderful philosophy indeed!" Swamiji remarked with a naughty smile in his face.

Swamiji points out that sense-control does not mean inability to enjoy the objects through the senses due to old age and other reasons, when you have lost the power of seeing, hearing, etc.

Sense-control in the real sense is to withdraw the senses from the sense objects with your will even when there is proper functioning of all the senses.

Sense-control leads one to mind control.

Mind control leads one to self-control. Self-control in turn leads one to Self-realisation.

28th APRIL 1959

BE SWEET

When Swamiji reached the office it was 10 a.m. today. Sri X came with letters for Swamiji's signature.

"Oji whenever you write letters, write sweetly. Don't give a cut and dry reply." Swamiji advised him.

"Yes Swamiji I will do."

"What you will do?.....How many times have I told you about this? Still you don't try to correct yourself. Very good. Take one Jilebi." Swamiji asked.

He took one Jilebi and tested it.

"How is it? very sweet!" Swamiji asked.

"Yes Swamiji, it is very sweet," came the reply.

"See. After all this Jilebi is insentient. How much happiness it gives to man. Whereas you are a human being with an intellect. How much more happiness you should give to others through your words and actions?" Swamiji mildly reproached him.

Sri X felt a little hurt. Immediately Swamiji turned to a visitor.

"You know, this Swamiji translates all my articles and sends them to various vernacular magazines ....Very energetic, sincere and honest . . . ." Swamiji praised him to the top.

Again Sri X's face became normal.

"Acchaji, take one more Jilebi. Your next letter must be more sweet than this Jilebi. You can go now. Namah Sivaya."

This is a unique method of Swamiji to correct an aspirant whenever one repeats the same mistake often. Swamiji will point out his mistake, in the midst of all visitors, and make him feel ashamed of himself. But the moment he repents for it, Swamiji starts praising him to the top and makes him forget the blow given to his ego.

Thus Swamiji uses this sugar-coated quinine doses on Sadhaks once in a way for their own improvement.

29th APRIL 1959

SWAMIJI. . . THE SOLACE OF THE POOR

A blind man who was sitting in a corner, approached Swamiji and prostrated before him.

"Swamiji, by your grace I am able to sing and play violin also. I have none in this world to look after me. You are my only solace now. I pray for thy blessings,"—the blind man politely requested Swamiji with folded hands.

You all know what could have been the reply of the ever-compassionate Swamiji.

Immediately he was admitted as an inmate of the Ashram.

Someone said that the blind man knows by heart, all the ten Upanishads and the whole of Bhagavad Gita.

"Is it not a blessing, Swamiji, he has such talents, even though he is blind?" Sri Tejomal, a devotee from Indonesia remarked.

"Yes. That is God's Grace. When you become absolutely helpless, God's Grace comes there for your help," Swamiji replied.

Then Swamiji asked Satyagnanam to arrange for his stay and food, etc.

Swamiji's absolute surrender to the Almighty's Will is something magnanimous and most wonderful, unimaginable and inexpressible. his unshakable conviction in the Divine Plan is such, he never bothers about the morrow and leaves it entirely in the hands of the Lord.

Whoever comes taking refuge in Swamiji, is given admission in the Ashram. Almost everyday there will be one or two new inmates. Swamiji never bothers about the pecuniary condition of the Ashram. Secretaries are puzzled as how to maintain this ever increasing number.

Once when the secretary complained the situation to Swamiji that it was impossible to maintain any more inmates due to the Ashram's inadequate income, Swamiji gave an answer which reflected his inner conviction in the Divine Will.

"Oji, whenever a new man comes here to stay permanently, know that God has sent his food and other needs already here in advance. So you need not worry about that. The moment he goes from here, the food also will go wherever he goes, before him. So be calm. Go and do Japa."

This was the answer Swamiji gave him.

On so many occasions, the Ashram had faced grave situation and had suffered even for the day's food. The secretaries found no solution except to think of sending away all and stop all the activities. Even then Swamiji's reply was this.

"If God wants that His work should continue in this world through this Ashram, He will take care of its maintainence also. It is His look after and not ours. If at all He does not want it, we will close the Ashram. Take Biksha. Sit and do Japa and Meditation. That is all. So, don't worry. Everything will become alright" Swamiji pacified all.

Are not all these, golden words of wisdom, which illumine, elevate and inspire us?

The most mysterious thing was, the second day after this talk someone sent a big donation in thousands for the Ashram's maintainence without our appeal or request.

The secretary ran to Swamiji to convey news about the donation received, with joy in his face. But he got a shock when Swamiji said that the major portion of the amount received, should be utilised for printing some more unpublished manuscripts.

Is it not a wonder?

Yes. Everything is a wonder here.

Swamiji is a wonder. Sivanandashram is a wonder. Sivanandanagar is a wonder. Publishing 5 books in a month, which is not heard of even in big institutions anywhere, is another wonder. Distribution of free books worth lakhs is one more wonder. Wonder of wonders is Swamiji's moulding of human into Divine.

1st MAY, 1959

EXISTENCE-CONSCIOUSNESS IS BLISS

It was 9-30 a.m. Swamiji's Kutir was opened. Swamiji was sitting in his sofa, outside the Varandah. Dr. Sivananda Hridayananda was standing behind him. Sri Swami Satchidananda was sitting down by the side of Swamiji with the letters. Swami Venkatesanandaji entered, and prostrated before Swamiji.

"Self is Satchidananda, Existence-consciousness-bliss. Existence is consciousness, but how can you say that it is bliss also?" Swamiji enquired Sri Venkateshanandaji.

Then Swamiji himself answered after a pause,

"All men in this world are in constant search of happiness and bliss everlasting. But they don't get it in these temporal things of the world. Man tries for this happiness and bliss in all the objects of the world and still he feels a sense of want. But a sage who has realised his Self or Atma which is existence and consciousness ever rests contented and peaceful. He is not in search of any more bliss anywhere. This proves that Self is Existence, consciousness and bliss. Moreover, the Self is not blissful, but bliss itself. There is no enjoyer to enjoy the bliss. He becomes the Bliss Itself."

THE MIDDLE PATH

After the night Satsang, Sri Franz Von Poncet, a Sadhaka from South Africa who is staying in the Ashram for the past 5 months came near Swamiji to get some Prasad from his hands.

He looked very thin that one can count even his bones. He avoids taking even the necessary food for the body and meditates all the time. Noticing his poor health Swamiji advised him.

"Oji you must take care of your health. You should eat

131

well. Torturing the body is not Yoga. You will become so weak, you may not be able to sit for meditation even. "Yoga is not for the one who eats much and who does not eat at all." So don't go to extremes. Be moderate. Follow the golden medium. Eat well. Do some exercises both morning and in the evening. In no way this is going to obsturuct your meditation.

On the other hand, Asans and exercises will help your meditation".

Swamiji always stresses much importance in the maintenence of the Sadhakas' health. He not only writes about this but practically demonstrates in his own daily life.

"Whatsoever a great man does, that the other men also do. Whatever he sets up as a standard, that the people follow."

Even today Swamiji has his routine Asans, Pranayama, and some bed exercises. He does all these things, to inspire Sadhakas to have a regulated disciplined life, to elevate them by his own examples, and not to gain anything for himself.

For him there is nothing to attain or to achieve. He need not follow the 'means' still, because he has already reached the goal.

INWARD COMMUNION

Swamiji was about to start to his Kutir. One gentleman came there.

"Swamiji I want to have a private talk with you, Will you please allow me now?"

"Talk to yourself" Swamiji got up and started moving towards his Kutir.

Don't think, 'talking to oneself' is the action of a mad-cap. Talking to yourself, Swamiji means, is to enquire about yourself. If the enquiry goes serious, then comes the discovery of your SELF. Automatically it ends in recovery.

THOU ART THAT

The morning sun spreads his mild rays, peeps through the mountain range, welcomes, Swamiji, the light of the Himalayas, as soon as he emerges out from his Kutir everyday.

These days Swamiji comes to the office by 6 o'clock in the morning and returns by 7-30.

When Swamiji was attending to his routine work in the office, Sri Elizabeth, an aspirant from America who is staying in the Ashram, came to the office, took her seat in the sofa in front of Swamiji.

"What is the nature of Absolute?" proceeded the question from Swamiji.

"Infinite, perfection," came the hesitating reply from her.

"Is not the same your nature also?" again Swamiji asked.

"No, Swamiji, how can it be? I am changing."

"You are not changing, only your teeth change, your body changes. But you are the Changeless Essence, The Self, the Silent witness of all these changes," Swamiji corrected her.

"Swamiji, but unless I experience how can I say so".

"Of course. But you must know theoretically first. Then only you can put it into practice." Swamiji replied.

Swamiji points out that theoretical knowledge is essential for anything so that it can be put into practice. Unless one knows theory of a particular subject, it is impossible for him to put it into practice in the right way.

Theoretical knowledge without practising it becomes useless, and dry philosophy. Practice without having a correct knowledge of theory, cannot give you the right result.

Therefore learn, learn well, and then put into practice what you have learnt.

SILENCE OF SPEECH

An young Sannyasi came to Swamiji. Swamiji gave him some books. He showed one book, and made some signs and gestures with his hands. Nobody could understand what he meant by that. Then took a slate and wrote that he is observing Mouna and he wants Swamiji's autograph in a book.

Swamiji turned to him.

"Oji, leave this kind of silence. Silence the mind. That is more important."

Suddenly Swamiji started showing some signs and gestures with his hands and acted as if one who observes Mouna.

All enjoyed the joke and burst into laughter but no one could understand what Swamiji meant.

Then Swamiji himself cleared it.

"A Sadhu who was observing silence stood before a house. He wanted a cup of milk and for this purpose he made all sort of signs as I showed you just now. What a waste of energy? What is the use of observing this kind of silence. Instead of telling, just a word, that he wants milk, he will be struggling to make that man understand what he needs, for ten minutes, wasting his own time and energy and as well as of the householder.

Silence the mind. Silence the thoughts. Silence the bubbling emotions. Silence the Vrittis. Rest in Silence and that is real silence.

REALITY OF THIS WORLD

Sri Santosh entered the office, and approached Swamiji straight away.

"Swamiji, is the world real or unreal," Santosh put a question.

"From the Absolute standpoint the world is unreal. But it

is relatively real. That is Vyavahara Satta. It is a solid reality for a worldly man. It is like a burnt cloth for a Jivanmukta. For a Viveki it loses its charms and attractions," replied Swamiji.

FOR A TV APPEARNCE IN EUROPE

It was morning 5-15. The morning sun was rising up quickly to chase away the darkness all around.

That was the time, many of the inmates used to have their bath in the Ganges. They were coming, one by one to the Ganges bank. Each one had a sweet shock when they came near the office building. They were surprised to see Swamiji sitting calmly with serene composure, all alone, in front of the office.

The previous day Mr. Loursais, a French documentary film director came here, and wanted to take the activities of the Ashram in movie film for broadcasting the same all over France and Switzerland, through Television, and the programme was fixed today morning. That was the reason for Swamiji's surprising early appearance.

Whenever a programme is fixed, one can see Swamiji as the first person on the scene, even before the work starts. Such presence of Swamiji always works an encouragement and inducement for the Sadhaks and inmates to discharge their duties with pleasure.

It is this quality, that the modern administrative officers, should learn from Swamiji.

Within half an hour everything was arranged. Mr Loursais started his outdoor shooting on the banks of the Ganges and the Himalayas as the background view. Satsang with Swamiji's Kirtan and Bhajan, a five-Veena recital and a Pada Pooja were shot by Mr. Loursais.

The shooting came to a close at about 11 a.m. and Swamiji returned to his Kutir.

2nd MAY, 1959

INTERVIEW WITH SIVANANDA

After finishing the office work Swamiji proceeded towards the eye hospital where another scene was to be shot by Mr Loursais, this morning. When Swamiji with his devotees entered the hospital, we found not the eye hospital there, but a studio with lighting and camera settings.

The scene was an interview with Swamiji. Mr Loursais put some questions to Swamiji regarding the Ashram activities, divine life, religion, etc. The whole scene was shot with sound recording.

Here is the actual picture I will place before you. Kindly listen to it.

Camera Man: Silence Please... .Put off the fans .... Lights on. .. .Camera rolling. . . .

Mr Loursais comes, bows to Swamiji and takes his seat in front of Swamiji. Swamiji greets him.

Swamiji: Welcome Mr. Loursais. . . .Om Namo Narayanaya. Hail Hail Jesus.

Loursais: Thank you Swamiji. Glad to meet you. I have heard much about you. Swamiji, could you please tell us a few words in French?

Swamiji: O Yes. "Kamasava, Banjore, Trabiyang."

Loursais: Swamiji, You are a well-learned scholar. Could you please tell me how many books have you written?

Swamiji: About three hundred books.

Loursais: On what subjects?

Swamiji: Religion, philosophy, ethics, health, etc.

136

Loursais: Thank you very much, Swamiji. I have read you have many titles. Can you please say what they are?

Swamiji: I am a Swami, a Paramahamsa Sannyasi. Therefore I have no titles.

Loursais: That is very nice. Swamiji, what is Paramahamsa?

Swamiji: Paramahamsa means a pure, perfect Sannyasi of the highest order.

Loursais: Swamij, what are the essential objects of your Divine Life Society?

Swamiji: Dissemination of spiritual knowledge, training of the aspirants in Yoga and Vedanta, etc. and selfless service to humanity.

Loursais: Swamiji, it seems you have introduced a separate system of philosophy, is it not?

Swamiji: It is not a separate system. It is a combination and a well regulated form of all the existing systems of Karma Yoga, Bhakti Yoga, Raja Yoga and Jnana Yoga. It is called the Yoga of Synthesis.

Loursais: Why did you put it in that way, Swamiji?

Swamiji: Because it is the only system which is best suited for the modern man. By following this Yoga of Synthesis one gets an integral development of personality, i.e. one develops his head, heart, hands and mind simultaneously. Karma Yoga purifies, Bhakti Yoga broadens the heart, Raja Yoga steadies the mind and Jnana Yoga gives the final illumination.

Loursais: Swamiji, you say that the goal of life is Self-realisation. What is it?

Swamiji: Well asked Mr. Loursais. Man realises his essential divine nature that he is the All-pervading immortal Soul, birthless, deathless, changeless and decayless.

Loursais: How do we know that a man is realised or not?

Swamiji: Yes you can know. Such man will be fearless, desireless, egoless and have a balanced mind in pleasure and pain, heat and cold.

Loursais: Who is a Swami?

Swamiji: Who loves all, serves all, shares with all what he has.

Loursais: Can I become a Swami, then? Swamiji: O yes, Why not. Anybody can become a Swami.

Loursais: Swamiji, could you please tell me what role can the Sadhu play for the progress of the nation?

Swamiji: They can do selfless service, they can become spiritual teachers and spread the gospel of divine life in the country, they can take part in the social works also.

Loursais: Swamiji, are you following only the religion of Rama and Krishna?

Swamiji: I have here the Universal Religion. I embrace all religions. All religions are one, because the essentials of all religions are one and the same. All religions say, there is God. Love all, serve all, be kind to all.

Loursais: Swamiji, can a Christian become a Swami?

Swamiji: O yes. He can become a Swami, if he likes. The Christian Fathers, Muslim Fakirs, Buddha Bikhshus are all the same order like that of a Sannyasi of the Hinduism.

Loursais: What do you think of Lord Jesus?

Swamiji: He is the supreme Lord. He is an incarnation of God. He said "I and my father are one." I respect him. I adore him as Rama and Krishna and Buddha.

Loursais: Do you celebrate Christmas here in your Ashram?

Swamiji: O yes. On a very grand scale with Christmas tree, Carol songs, Christmas cakes, etc.

Loursais: O it is something wonderful, to see Christmas being celebrated in an Indian Ashram. Swamiji, do you sing any song on Lord Jesus?

Swamiji: O yes. Hear this:

"O my Jesus, O Lord Jesus, hail hail Jesus, O Father Father.

O my Mary, O virgin Mary, hail hail Mary, O Mother Mother."

Loursais: Thank you very much Swamiji. I am indebted you.

Swamiji garlands him and blesses him. Thus ends the shooting.

THIRST FOR KNOWLEDGE OR CURIOSITY

Sri Ananda Narayan Vyas, an advocate from Allahabad had an interesting conversation with Swamiji, today in the office.

"When the crucification was ordered, Jesus said, 'Why hast thou forsaken me Father' and just before the crucification he said, 'forgive them Father, they don't know what they do'. Why he has said these contradictory statements, Swamiji?" the advocate asked.

"Do not bother to analyse great men's actions. They are transcendental. Our ordinary mind cannot understand those mysteries. Instead of trying to analyse the "Why and What" of those statements, why can't you try to follow at least one of his many sayings?" Swamiji replied.

"What is Brahmacharya, Swamiji?" the advocate asked.

"Brahmacharya is Purity," replied Swamiji.

"What do you mean by purity, Swamiji? It is a difficult term to understand."

"Purity is freedom from sensual desires," replied Swamiji.

"Is not physical purity necessary Swamiji?"

"Mental purity automatically brings forth physical purity also, therefore one should try to purify the mind first."

"What is goodness, Swamiji?" proceeded the next question.

"Goodness is God" Shantam, Subham, Sundaram. God is the Supreme Goodness" replied Swamiji.

Then the advocate started to ask some other doubts. Swamiji simply kept quiet. He never answered. After sometime someone brought Agarbatti, as an offering to Swamiji. Immediately Swamiji took one of them and gave it to the advocate. "Pray, all your doubts will be cleared."

The advocate accepted and stopped his queries.

Swamiji gives here a clue for the aspirants. Doubts can be cleared, not by solving it one by one, for, the human mind is such if one doubt is cleared another one will crop up and there will be no end for this process.

Cutting off the branches one by one is not the correct way to cut off the whole tree. The process is not to cut the branches, but strike at the root at a stretch. Then whole tree is rooted out.

Similarly trying to solve the doubts one by one is not the correct method. The one who is the cause for all these doubts should be rooted out, that is the impure Vasanas of the mind should be annihilated. The best method is surrender to the Divine.

As usual Swamiji was attending to his routine.

The purpose of prayer is to surrender your individual ego

at the feet of the Divine. Then automatically Divine Grace flows and all your doubts are cleared.

WHAT IS KARMA YOGA

Office work. Some one remarked that a certain politician has no faith in God.

Sri Atmaram interrupted him saying, "But he is doing wonderful Karma Yoga."

"What is Karma Yoga without faith in God. It is not Karma Yoga but mere Karma," Swamiji marked.

Yes it is true. How is it possible to do Karma Yoga unless one accepts the existence of God. Karma Yoga is to serve humanity with Atma Bhava or Narayana Bhava. Unless one has the Bhava that he serves the Lord in man how can Karma (actions) become Yoga. The very fundamental principle of Karma Yoga is to sublimate Karma (action) into Yoga, that is, by following the method of Karma Yoga, one's action becomes, the means to attain union with the Lord. Swamiji gives the gist of Karma Yoga in a concentrated tablet form. He says "Remember three "N." This is Karma Yoga Sadhana." The first 'N' is Nimitta Bhava, i.e., to have the attitude that you are an instrument in the hands of the Lord. The second 'N' is Narayana Bhava, i.e., to have the attitude that you serve Lord Narayana in all these forms. The third 'N' is Narayana Arpanamastu, i.e., to offer the fruits of your actions to the Lord.

Therefore to say "I have no faith in God, but do Karma Yoga" is absurd.

Then Dr. V. said "Nowadays politicians think that they become politicians only if they make such statements in a public platform."

"Yes all these things will be there so far man is hale and hearty. If he gets 'ARTHRITIS' then you ill see, what he is. At that time he will cry out,

"O Lord Save me." Swamiji smilingly remarked.

DOUBT ABOUT THE DOUBTER

Swamiji was going through a manuscript. Suddenly he turned to Swami Lalithanandaji, an American disciple.

"Can you doubt the doubter" Swamiji asked her.

"Yes....Swamiji" hesitatingly she said.

"You have failed. .. .Now the next question..., I will see whether you get pass mark now. .. .They say that everything is illusion. This whole world is unreal, a mere illusion. If every-thing is illusion your Brahman also is an illusion. How can you say that Brahman alone is real? Is it correct?"

"Brahman is beyond illusion" Swami Lalithananda replied.

"No that is not the correct answer. There must be a substratum for the illusory snake. That substratum is the rope. So the rope cannot be an illusion. So also Brahman is the substratum for this illusory world. The world alone is illusion and not the substratum, the Brahman. It is real. Moreover, the one who denies everything else as illusion cannot be denied. He exists. He is Real. Therefore Brahman alone is real. This world is unreal and illusion. It is superimposed on Brahman. Understood, Swami Lalithanandaji?" Swamiji corrected her by the above answer.

CHIDANANDA RUPA SIVOHAM

A Sadhu came and stood before Swamiji. He was going on repeating 'Sivoham Sivoham.'

Whenever he repeated Sivoham, Swamiji said, "Dasoham."

But he was going on repeating "Sivoham Sivoham."

Swamiji called Satyajnanam. "Oji, take off the Kamandalu from that Sadhu."

Sri Satyajnanam approached him. The Sadhu immediately said holding the Kamandalu with a firm grip, "Maharaj, this Kamandalu is my life. I cannot part with it."

"See, the true colour of the "Sivoham" has come out now. Oji, don't say Sivoham, say, "Kamandaloham"! Swamiji said smilingly. All burst into laughter.

10th June, 1959

ANATOMY OF THE SOUL

"Where are you coming from?"

"From Madurai, Swamiji. My name is Sarada. I am preparing now for the M.Sc. Anatomy."

"Oh that is wonderful. What is histology?" "Histology is the science of the cells."

"Oh, you are a very bright student! Do you know the anatomy of the Soul?"

"No Swamiji."

"I will tell you. Listen. The first is Annamaya Kosha. Then you find Pranamaya Kosha, behind it there are Manomaya and Vijnanamaya Koshas, and then you find Anandamaya Kosha. Transcending all these Koshas there shines the Soul, the birthless, deathless, changeless, immortal entity. This is the anatomy of the Soul. Understood now?"

"Yes, Swamiji, thanks."

A RIDDLE FOR
THE TOP-MAN IN EACH PROFESSION

The above was a conversation which took place, in the office this morning between Swamiji and a visitor from Madurai.

This is Swamiji's unique method of imparting spiritual knowledge to the various kinds of men and women of all fields of life, by asking questions according to the taste in their particular field in which they are accustomed. It becomes easier then for the visitor to swallow the bitter spiritual pills and digest them without much difficulty.

To a famous surgeon for whom major operations are mere child's play, Swamiji puts a test by asking "How many

Ego-dectomy you have performed?" and makes him look on the rafters, for, the famous surgeon has never even heard any such 'Dectomy" in his medical science.

After a pause, to the astonishment of the onlooker Swamiji explains the "Ego-dectomy" performjng which one is cured of, the abscess of ignorance, the root-cause of all the pains and sufferings of the world.

An efficient engineer who has constructed number bridges may come to Swamiji with pride in his face.

"Are you an engineer? That is wonderful. Tell me how to build the bridge of immortality?" will be a sweet shocking question, which makes the engineer stand-still.

Perhaps the famous engineer would not have been aware of the fact that Swamiji, the Divine Doctor, would also be a Divine Engineer who is an expert in constructing the bridge of Immortality across the turbulent river of Samsara by walking on which one reaches the abode of bliss eternal.

Don't think there ends the matter.

A well reputed chartered accountant, who came to Swamiji, stood wonderstruck and thought within, "What! I am auditing the accounts of big firms whereas this Swamiji audits myself."

The reason is, when he introduced himself as an auditor "Audit yourself and check your balance sheet" was the advice of Swamiji to him.

One should not think that Swamiji's unique method of imparting knowledge in these ways is meant only for the educated masses. He can even come to the level of an illiterate man and make him understand sublime truths of the Upanishads, through homely examples. Listen to this conversation, which took place in his Kutir when he was having his lunch.

"Krishna, today you have prepared the dishes very nicely.

Oh, what a wonderful 'Pachadi' you have prepared (Pachadi is a curd preparation). Krishna, how do I know the taste of this 'Pachadi'? Can you tell?"

"Through your tongue, Swamiji", Krishna replied.

"No, listen what happens. See, first I take a little and put it on the tip of my tongue. The tongue gives this news to the mind. Mind is the lawyer. The mind now takes it to intellect. The intellect is the judge. Behind the intellect is the Supreme Court Judge, God, who is Asti, Badhi, Priya, i.e. existence, knowledge, bliss. He gives the power to decide the taste to the intellect, mind and the tongue.

Therefore, God gives the tongue the power of taste, to the mind the power of thinking, and to the intellect the power of determining. Have you heard this before", have you understood now?"

"Swamiji, this is the first time I have understood it in this way."

Such is the greatness of Swamiji in giving experessions to the age-old scriptural teachings in his own original way applicable to one and all.

Moreover Swamiji's teachings are not from a mounted platform or only to a congregation. Whatever splits from his mouth will certainly be a spiritual gem, whenever and wherever it be. If you sincerly seek it, you will certainly find it.

I AM BLISS

"Shantanandaji, come here, what is the universal disease?" Swamiji asked and he himself answered.

"Jealousy and envy."

"How is the self an embodiment of Bliss."

Again Swamiji himself answered. "You like a mango because it gives you pleasure when you eat it. Besides everything else in this world, everybody likes himself most. Therefore Self must be happiness, i.e., it should be an embodiment of Bliss."

"Namahshivaya. Take this mango. You can go now."

These are all Swamiji's occasional flashes of wisdom.

The inner Wisdom flashes through his genuine smile, straight goes into the aspirant, illumines his heart, comes back once again, and settles in himself.

14th June, 1959

THE ONE AS MANY

Sri Nagarajan from Dehra Dun came with his family for Swamiji's Darshan this morning. An young boy, a relative of Sri Nagarajan, who plays Mridangam well, was there in the group.

"Who is this boy?" Swamiji asked Sri Nagarajan.

"He is the Brother of Shyama, Swamiji, who came here and gave a dance performance last year."

Then he introduced an old man as his father-in-law and told he is the grand father of this young boy.

"The same person you call him as father-in-law, the boy calls him grandfather and for your wife he is father."

"Similarly the One Omnipotent, Omnipresent, Omnicient Lord is called 'Hari' by one, Brahman by other and Father in Heaven by another and Allah by a fourth man. The person is the same, names are different. God is One. Truth is One. He is called by so many names."

LOOK WITH THE BLIND EYE

Pada Puja was arranged. Sri Kamala and Sri Santosh are performing the Pada Puja. They have ordered for a Garland of white Flowers. But it did not come in time. There was a Garland with mixed yellow and white flowers.

Sri Bhagyalakshmi Ammal who was present there told "Swamiji, if we remove the yellow flowers from the garland then it will become white garland."

"Why to remove the yellow flowers. Don't look at the yellow flowers. Then it becomes white garland." Swamiji remarked.

It may look for the onlooker as if Swamiji made a casual

148

remark. But go deeper you will find a beautiful practical philosophy behind it.

Varieties of things are there in this world with various names and forms, each one possessing different qualities, colour and taste.

Many a thing we like. Many a thing we hate. Sometimes we even grumble why God has created such and such an object which we dislike. But every thing in this world from an ant to an elephant is created with a definite purpose. Everything in this world will be of some use to some one in some way for some purpose.

That which you dislike and hate may be the essential need of another man. One man's meat is another man's poison.

Therefore the best method we have to adopt in this world to lead a harmonious worryless life, is just to withdraw our mind from those objects which are not suitable for our tastes and temperaments.

Swamiji's remark, "Don't look at an object, then it does not exist for you", clearly indicates that the object has no existence unless you give existence for it.

Therefore if you happened to come across an undesirable object, simply withdraw your mind. Then you will not be affected by the undesirable quality of that object.

You see now, in a sage's simple remark, what an ocean's depth of meaning is there! So don't be in the surface. Dive deep, you will get pearls of wisdom.

REJECT NOT, CRAVE NOT

"Hridayananda, take this sweets", Swamiji offered a handful of sweets.

"No Swamiji, I have already got it."

"Doesn't matter. Take this also. Reject not anything. At the same time crave for nothing." Swamiji replied.

Then Hridayanandaji accepted the sweets, Swamiji gave her.

You can master all the Upanishads and Brahma Sutras. You may be well read in all the bombastic writings and Shakespearian style of all the modern philosophers and reputed writers. But unless they are for any practical application in our daily life, they are mere words and become useless.

A friend of mine once came to me, showing me a book by a famous author on "Philosophy of Life," and admired "Sir what a beautiful style and expression! Who can write one sentence for five pages like this author. What a depth of knowledge he has got!"

"Of course, what you say about the author is cent per cent correct. But my dear friend, how far those bombastic style, beautiful expression, and one sentence for five pages help you in your daily life? What to do as soon as you get up from the bed? How can you chart out your daily routine by reading such books? For such things you have to exclusively read Swami Sivananda's writings. His is not a philosophy of words but a methodical philosophy given in a simple sweet practical manner following which all the problems of life can be solved, a life of peace harmony and bliss can be lived.

Now I come to the point. "Reject not anything, but crave for nothing."

According to your merits, circumstances and environments, comforts and conveniences are coming forth to you in their own accord. Therefore Swamiji says "Reject not whatever comes to you." Because the very act of rejection produces bondage. At the same time be careful, the acceptance of objects should not produce in you a craving for them, for, even then the craving is a bondage. The "I" ness and mine-ness in you makes you reject or crave for an object which is the root-cause of bondage. So Swamiji says, "Be a witness, whatever comes to you let it come, whatever goes from you let it go. Watch the drama of life, move happily unaffected by the pairs of opposites, pain and pleasure, honour and dishonour."

My friend, is not Swamiji's life's philosophy a living philosophy!

Here is another example.

"Krishna, do you want this silk cloth," Swamiji enquired Sri Krishna.

"No Swamiji", he said, but after a while, "Swamiji I will see it first and then say" he said.

"No, No. Once if you don't want it, don't look at it also. Because if you look at it, you' will get the desire to possess it also." Swamiji replied.

In Sivanandanagar you will get three kinds of feast daily. The first feast will be in the Kitchen as you all know. The second one, you get for your intellect during the discourses and lectures in the Satsang. The third and the most valuable feast is the feast for your heart and soul, you get it from Swamiji himself.

For the other two feasts you have to exert, but for this feast you need not, because even without your knowledge Swamiji fills your heart and soul with his precious spiritual advices.

Swamiji told Sri Nitya Kumari Rani of Nepal.

"A Sadhak should develop his heart in two ways. He must be hard-hearted and as well soft-hearted. Hard-hearted when you stick to your principles, when you stick to a particular aim and the same hard heart should melt in compassion like butter when you see the suffering of a poor man on the road side."

TRUE EDUCATION

Prof. Sri Sahanani from Delhi had come to have Swamiji's

Darshan this morning in the office. He took his seat, after prostrating Swamiji.

"Sri Sahanani Maharaj, see, this is Pushpanand Vice Principal Dehra Dun, this is Savitri M.A., this is Principal Killo from Delhi, that is Kusum another professor from Delhi." Swamiji introduced them all to Sri Sahanani.

"Full of educationists but everywhere you find only ignorance" Swamiji significantly remarked.

Swamiji points out the futility of the empirical knowledge of the world. What avail are they, Swamiji asks, unless they help you to gain the supreme knowledge of the self knowing which the sorrows and tribulations of the world are put an end to? M.A., M.Sc, Ph.D. and D. Litt are the degrees which you strive for, only increase your worries and anxieties to the superlative degree and nothing else. Your Ph.D. only helps to search for a professorship in a college which pays a petty amount of few hundred rupees.

Is not such knowledge, in that case, mere ignorance?

In one of his books Swamiji defines the true education thus.

"That education which makes you tread the path of truth, and righteousness, which moulds your character, which helps you to attain freedom, perfection and knowledge of the Self and at the same time enables you to make out an honest living can be called TRUE EDUCATION."

Therefore O Man! gain not the knowledge which is ignorance, but the knowledge which leads you to the wisdom of the Self.

BE SIMPLE BUT INSTRUCTIVE

Swamiji was going through a letter typed by an inmate.

Suddenly his face beamed with smile, he turned towards the devotees who were present there.

"Oji, see, here is a letter which contains some instructions to a student. It is a reply to a devotee's letter. It reads, "Stick to your guns." What is this "stick to your guns." Does it mean "stick to your principles and resolves?"

Swamiji said and further remarked.

People nowadays think that it is inferior to write simple English. It is a sad mistake. The purpose of writing is to make the reader understand it clearly without any difficulty and follow it. What is the use of writing bombastic phrases and figures of speech, to understand which a man has to go in search of a dictionary. Do you know, Atmaramji, "May Lord Pickle you." It is a funny story. Once a Governor was to inspect a school. The teacher told the students to greet the Governor, "May Lord preserve your Excellency." One among the students who thought the word "Preserve" a simple one, and wanted to put a big term instead of that. So when the Governor entered he greeted "May Lord pickle your Excellency." (laughter)

So such will be the end result of using phrases and figures of speech to the common man.

Write simple sentences and make your point clear to the reader. Then he will be benefited and at the same time your purpose of writing also will be fulfilled.

The Silence prevailed in the office hall for few minutes seemed that the devotees had accepted his advice which was given in his unique simple language.

TO DEFINE GOD . . . .

Swamiji was in the office with his usual routine work. Sri Veera Burch an American devotee of Swamiji entered the office and prostrated before Swamiji. She took her seat.

"How is your dysentery now? Do you feel alright?" Swamiji kindly enquired.

"Yes Swamiji....I am alright now."

"I will give you an Indian Name. ... You are 'Mira' from to-day. Do you know 'Mira'. . . .a great woman saint of India?"

"Yes Swamiji I have read...."

"What is the best possible definition of God?" Swamiji enquired.

"……………"

"Dr. Sushila! Can you tell?"

"Satchidananda is the best definition of God."

Do you know why Swamiji has put a significant remark in his question, "Best possible definition?"

Yes. There is a hidden meaning behind it.

Because God cannot be defined. God can be very well recognised by what He is not, than by what He is, for, He is infinite, beyond speech, mind and intellect. He is a Limitless Being. We can define a finite object, but how can we define an infinite limitless being? To define God is to limit the limitless Being, that is, to confine God in the concepts of mind which cannot be the Absolute Truth about God.

Then in that case what is the way to understand Him and attain Him.

Positive descriptions about God have been given by sages just in order to make the aspirant understand so that he can meditate on Him. "God is infinite" sages declared because the aspirant may misunderstand Him as finite. But in reality He is beyond finite and infinite.

"God is Light" because one should not think of Him as darkness. But in fact He is beyond Light and darkness which one can understand after realisation.

These are all relative descriptions which do not exist in God.

Therefore the best possible definition of God is Sat-Chit-Ananda. He is Existence Absolute, Knowledge Absolute, Bliss Absolute.

To make it clear that He is not Asat (Non existence) they said He is Sat; He is not Jada (Inert) so they said He is Chit (Consciousness); He is not Duhkha (pain) so they said He is Bliss. In reality God is beyond Sat and Asat, Chit and Jada, Duhkha and Ananda.

MAYA

"Sri Mira, who is the most cunning woman jugler in New York?" A wave of naughty smile was dancing in Swamiji's face when he asked the question.

"In New York?" Sri Mira was puzzled.

"Can you say, Dr. Sushila" Swamiji enquired.

"............."

"Can you say Dr. Hridayananda.".

"............."

Swamiji himself answered. "She is Maya"

"Why in 'New York' Swamiji, she is everywhere." Someone raised an objection.

"If I ask simply, it is very easy, any body will reply. So I added, 'in New York'." Swamiji replied and smiled.

All burst into laughter.

DIVINE DOCTOR'S DIAGNOSIS

A middle aged person came to Swamiji.

"Swamiji, I want to go back home."

"What? yesterday you told you want to stay here. Now you tell you want to go back. What happened to you?"

"No Swamiji. I often fall ill. I am a diseased man."

"Oji, think that I will die at any moment. No disease will come to you. Further if you have bank balance, you will get disease. If you are penniless no disease will come unto you.

What is this! This Doctor Swamiji's diagnosis looks something new! How can the disease come when there is bank balance! One may wonder. But it is a truth.

The money and property which you possess are God-given, entrusted to you by God to spend it in charity to the poor and the needy. But man's selfishness makes him forget this law. He stores the money without utilising it for good purposes.

How to bring out the money which is in the bank, useful for none?

The Nature's work starts. It gives the person some acute disease. Famous specialists, physicians and surgeons attend on him. 10 injections, 4 ointments, 5 mixtures daily. .. .Consulting fees Rs. 100. Attending fees daily Rs. 100, medicine charges in thousands. .. .within a short time the bank account shows nil balance.

The person, who was hesitating to give one Naya Pysa for a poor man, now is ready to spend any amount on doctors. Such is the law. You cannot escape from it.

Therefore "O man!" Swamiji warns, "Do not store up the God-given property. You are only an agent. Spend it in charity. Share with all. Give. Give. You will acquire the wealth of God. But if you fail to do this due to selfishness, then nature will compel you to spend it in all evil ways and add more sin to your account."

26th July, 1959

THE SAGE'S EXPERIENCE

"Namasthe" Swamiji, we are all Social Education Officers. We have come to have your Darshan.

A group of middle aged persons came and bowed to Swamiji.

"Very glad, take these books,"

"Swamiji, we want a message from you" one of them asked.

"Serve, Love, Give, Meditate, Realise, Be Good, Do good" Swamiji gave his message in the form of consecrated divine Pills.

"Swamiji, the world is too materialistic now. It is very difficult to practise these things" one of them remarked.

"Oji, this world was much more materialistic in Ravana's time. It is much more better now. "Swamiji replied.

"You are a Bengali? "Swamiji enquired someone in the group.

"O Swamiji, we have forgotten to introduce ourselves."

"Doesn't matter. . . .You are all in me. . . .Mr. Gupta, Mr. Naidu, Mr. Sharma, Mr. Dave, Mr. Chopra all are in me only......

Swamiji made this remark with a relaxation. "But you don't know me Sir, I am Oriya man," someone said.

"O Yes, I know you also even before you came here" Swamiji replied with a smile.

"All are in me." "I am in all" is the experience of a Jeevanmukta. Nothing is new, nothing is old, none is a stranger for Swamiji who has realised the ONE which shines in all.

Therefore there is no need of introducing who am I, who is he, for, Swamiji knows it already, who is who, what is who.

"Tell me, what is education? "Swamiji enquired one of them.

"Education is life."

To rest in God is education." Swamiji replied. Swamiji points out the true significance of real education.

"That education which paves the way to God and rest in Him is the real education."

THE PSYCHIATRIST IS ANALYSED

Swamiji was about to start back to his Kutir after the office work. Sri Bhagawa brought two Brazilian visitors and introduced them to Swamiji.

Swamiji entertained them with his usual hospitality.

Coffee and biscuits came. ...books in lot were distributed.

Western visitors in the Ashram were introduced to them.

In a short moment Swamiji made them feel homely.

The gentleman introduced himself as a psychiatrist.

"What is the source of the mind?" Swamiji asked him.

"No Swamiji, I don't know."

"The source of the mind is Soul or spirit. Mind is nothing but a bundle of thoughts, desires, cravings. Annihilate the desires and cravings, there is no mind. Then you can ever rest in peace, become one with the Spirit and enjoy the everlasting happiness.

Then the visitors were shown the exhibition, Eye Hospital, etc.

They departed with a contented heart.

SAHAJA SAMADHI

"Swamiji, when a man realises, how long he can keep that Realisation?" an old man approached Swamiji this morning in the office and asked the question.

After a Pause Swamiji replied.

"First there will be a glimpse. .. .it will last for a short time. Gradually he will be established in that State. Then it becomes Sahaja Avastha or Natural State."

The old man went back to his seat.

Sahaja Avastha or Natural State, Swamiji explains in one of his books, is a blessed State in which the sage has the effortless, unbroken awareness of the Reality or the Self all throughout, in all conditions, wherever he is, and whatever he does.

QUESTION-TIME

"Atmaramji, which quality embraces all other qualities?" Swamiji asked Atmaram who was sitting in front of Him.

Some replied Ahimsa and some replied Truth. "Humility," Swamiji himself gave the answer

Sri Santosh entered.

"What is the key to Divine Life?" proceeded the question from Swamiji's smiling face and gave a hearty welcome to Santosh.

"Right Thinking is the discrimination that the World is unreal replied...." she was thinking further to give the right answer.

"I am Immortal Soul" is right thinking, Swamiji replied.

After a Namaskar she returned.

"What are the three eyes of a Sadhak" Swamiji turned towards Dr. Susila.

No reply came from her.

"They are the Eye of discrimination, the Eye of devotion, the Eye of wisdom.

The Eye of discrimination perceives behind all phenomenal appearances, the One real which is changeless.

The Eye of devotion sees God and God alone in all beings.

The Eye of wisdom sees the One Satchidananda Brahman alone everywhere.

The Sadhak does not get all these three eyes all at once. First he gets the first two. They enable him the third Eye to open." When he gets the third Eye, the Eye of Wisdom, the Sadhak becomes a sage."

12th October, 1959

THE THREE 'K's

Swamiji was on his way to the office. It was about 10-30 in the morning. When he came near the main arch which leads to the office building, Sri Chandravati from Gaya who was waiting there for Swamiji's Darshan, prostrated before him.

"Aooji.... Chandravati. . . .tell me. . . .what are the three 'K's?

She expected the answer from Swamiji himself. "They are Kamini, Kanchana and Kirti (woman, gold and fame).

"How to overcome these three?" proceeded the next question from Swamiji. Again Swamiji himself gave the answer.

"Practise celibacy and conquer Kamini. Embrace poverty and conquer Kanchana. Develop humility and overcome Kirti."

It is not that, Swamiji means, that women by themselves are not a hinderance in the progress but it is the lust in man which becomes the block in the onward path of evolution. When you overcome lust by the practice of Brahmacharya, women cease to be women for you. To conquer over 'Kamini' is to conquer over Lust which can be done by the Practice of Brahmacharya.

Next, Kanchana (money) itself is not an obstruction but the desire for possession is a hindrance. By saying 'Embrace Poverty', Swamiji only means to lead a simple life having the bare necessities without craving or attachment for the wealth.

Fame comes to any man who is sincere, honest, truthful and works for the common good, Ieaving aside his selfish interest.

But the pity in most of the poeple is, that they forget all about their spirit of service and are carried away the moment they get a little name and fame. Then they use the very same field to acquire more and more fame.

But they are not aware that Selfishness has entered in them through the back door to spoil them.

One may think, and it may even appear to many that the work one does, seems to be only for the common good of the people. If it so the cause, such work when it is done in the right spirit without any expectation out of it, ought to have purified the person, and have made him soar high in the realm of spirituality. But what happens here is, that the very same work which appears to be selfless, becomes tainted with selfish motive in the course of time, because of that drawback, the desire for name and fame, the selfish motive behind such so-called selfless service. Therefore Swamiji warns us to be cautious and advises to develop humility along with other virtues. Humility is the greatest of virtues because in the absence of humility in a person, all other virtues, even though he may possess, are hidden from view and there is a chance of losing all other good qualities in due course because of the non-possession of this single virtue, humility. So, the three 'K's which Maya uses as baits to pull the Jivas are Kamini, Kanchana and Kirti. What is the way to overcome them? 1. Practise Brahmacharya. 2. Embrace poverty. 3. Develop humility.

1st January, 1960

HAPPY NEW YEAR

The Happy New Year dawned in Ananda Kutir today with the sacred Darshan of two Divine Souls.

Sri H.H. Swami Purushottamanandaji of Vashistha Guha visited the Ashram on his way to the plains, met Swamiji in his Kutir. Joy and peace pervaded the whole atmosphere.

One by one devotees and inmates came to Swamiji, prostrated before him and had his choicest blessings for the New Year. Swamiji conducted prayer, Maha Mrityunjaya Mantra for peace, prosperity and a bright New Year of the whole world.

After having a cup of milk Sri Swami Purushottamanandaji took leave of Swamiji.

COMFORTABLE VEDANTA

Swamiji graciously turned to the devotees and jovialy remarked:

"See, today is the first day of the New Year. If, everyone of you gives me something, yours will multiply like anything. Come on....Who comes first?"

Sri Pushpaji of Dehra Dun came forward and offered twenty rupees to Swamiji.

"What about you," Swamiji pointed to a devotee.

"These are all 'Anithya Vastu' (Temporal) Swamiji. Why to give all these things?" She replied.

"Comfortable Vedanta indeed! If you really feel they are Anithya, why don't you throw them away?" Swamiji remarked, all had a hearty laugh.

MANY WAYS AND ONE GOAL

"Why do you see diversity when there is really unity?" Swamiji put a question next.

"It is due to the illusory Power of God, Swamiji," Someone replied.

"Wonderful, tell me in one word the way to reach the goal" came the next question.

Each one gathered there gave different answers. "Faith" replied Sri Ramesh.

"Grace" replied Sri Gyanchand.

"Jnana", this is Vedantananda.

"Renunciation", this is Kalyani's reply. "Devotion" answered Sri Anasuya.

"Wonderful, all are correct" Swamiji remarked.

From the reply each one gives, one can understand the temperament and taste of that particular person. "Though men follow different paths according to their inborn nature yet they finally come to ME alone" says the Gitacharya.

Usually we see disciples of different temperaments, approach different Gurus suitable to each one of them in order to be guided through a particular path. But here in Anandakutir we see that thousands of aspirants all over the world with thousands of tastes and temperaments come to Swamiji and sit at His feet. Each one is satisfied though each one is of different make-up, for, he is moulded in his own way according to his wish.

Swamiji's teachings are not a particular set of dogmas of a certain creed or cult, belong to this religion or that religion, neither compels one to follow a particular faith nor converts one from one faith to another. His is the Universal, a synthetic approarh to reach the Goal which covers up the entire personality of an individual. That is why we find devotees and disciples are attracted to Swamiji's Sacred Feet.

TWENTIETH CENTURY RAMANUJA

Sri Srinivasan, an ardent devotee from Alleppy, a devotee who, at the very thought of having Swamiji's Darshan, simply flies from Kerala to Delhi, just to have Swamiji's Darshan and returns the same evening, came today to have Swamiji's blessings for the New Year. Swamiji blessed him.

In the midst of his talks Sri Srinivasan remarked, "Swamiji after the Great Ramanuja who initiated everyone irrespective of caste and creed, in the sacred 'Narayana' Mantra, I see only here, Swamiji pours out his Grace to one and all whether they want it or not. Nowhere I have heard Sannyasa Diksha given to persons as Swamiji bestows here. It is something thrilling to hear and see Swamiji's boundless mercy flowing to humanity. I have seen during the Auction, the auctioner will shout 'Going,.. Going' and when the people hesitate to buy the articles, he will shout 'Gone' and give up the entire lot. Similarly here Swamiji proclaims, "O ye aspirants, come on, I have wonderful thing for you to give. . . .come on. . . .It is going. .. .It is going ....Come quick and drink deep the divine Grace to your heart's content." But when the aspirants hesitate to come near, Swamiji never waits, he pulls them to his side and bestows on them the divine grace though they are not worthy of it."

All enjoyed Sri Srinivasa's humorous remark, but it is a fact of daily happening in Sivanandanagar.

After Pada Pooja by Ceylon devotees, the function came to an end.

4th January, 1960

SAGE AND YOGI

Today we had Swamiji's Darshan at about 10 a.m. Devotees came inside and took their seat after prostrating to Gurudev. Swamiji was going through a manuscript. A young German lady, seemed to be a seeker after salvation, just arrived at the Ashram, came near Swamiji and offered her respects.

"O. . . .Yes....Welcome ....Where do you come from?"

"I am coming from Germany Swamiji. ...I have heard of you through Sri Swami Swaroopananda, your German disciple there. He has sent his greeting to you."

"Thank you .... you have come at the correct time. ...take this hot coffee."

"Thanks, Swamiji, but I don't drink coffee. . .."

Then Swamiji gave her some fruits.

"Are you a Yogi or a sage?" Swamiji enquired of her.

"I don't know that, Swamiji, but I have come here for Self-realisation."

"That means you are a sage" Swamiji clarified the meaning of the two terms 'sage and 'Yogi' from the standpoint of Western aspirants. Although there is no difference between these two terms from the standpoint of the Truth, many of the western aspirants understand the term 'Yogi' to be the one who practises Asans, Pranayams, concentration and other exercises; the term sage to be the one who practises Vedantic method of reflection, enquiry, contemplation on the Absolute Truth. From the reply the young German lady gave, she seemed to be an aspirant of rational temperament.

THE WAYS OF THE LORD

"What is Lord's way?" Swamiji was holding a typed sheet on his hand and started asking questions from it.

No one replied and Swamiji himself replied. "Lord's way is mercy. Lord's language is Silence. Lord's food is the Egoism of man. Lord's ambassador is Guru.

Lord's gift is Self-knowledge. Lord's abode is the heart of devotees.

"Is not this German lady resembling Sri Surjit Singh of Dehra Dun, Swamiji ?" Sri Swami Sivananda Hridayanandaji remarked.

"Yes, yes, you have the image of Surjit in your mind and the reflection of it, you see through your mind on this lady and then she looks like Surjit Singh. That is the Truth." Swamiji replied, so to say, told the fact about perception.

Swamiji points out here a truth which we often miss to perceive and understand; that the name, form, quality and quantity we attribute to things outside are nothing but the reflection of our own mind inside. Whatever make the seeing subject, the same is the make of the object seen. When we see the world with the physical eyes, we see only gross objects. When we see through the mind, we conceive only ideas. When we see everything through the Self, we perceive Self alone everywhere. As is the mirror so is the reflection. Make the mind, the mirror, clean and steady and see the things outside. You will see everything Divine. This grand lesson Swamiji teaches us from his above mentioned remark.

MAHA VAKYAS

Sri Abinimohan Chakravarthy, an inmate of the Ashram approached Swamiji.

"Swamiji, 1 feel I have not understood the Mahavakyas

and their significance properly. I think, the Teacher points out to the disciple, Thou Art That (Tat Twam Asi) and then points him that this Self is Brahman (Ayam Atma Brahman). Then he realises It as I am Brahman (Aham Brahmasmi). Is not that correct Swamiji?"

"No. ... No .... It is not correct... .Now I will explain it to you. .. .Listen attentively."

Swamiji started explaining to him.

"The First Maha Vakya is 'Prajnanam Brahma' (Consciousness is Brahman). This is Lakshana Vakya. The teacher gives the definition to the student that pure consciousness is Brahman. Then he says, Thou Art That (Tat Twam Asi); you are that All-pervading Pure Consciousness. This is known as Upadesha Vakya. Then the student contemplates on what the teacher expounded, as 'Aham Brahmasmi' (I am Brahman). This is Anusandhana Vakya. Then finally he realises that this self which is within him is the Brahman (Ayamatma Brahma), this is Anubhava Vakya."

Have you understood now?

Thank you very much Swamiji. Abinimohan returned to his seat.

THEORY AND EXPERIENCE

A middle aged lady, a devotee from Ceylon who is working there as a Tamil Pandit was there sitting in front of Swamiji. Swamiji asked her to talk something in Tamil.

"About what?" She asked.

"About Self-knowledge and the way to reach it" Swamiji replied.

"Without having that experience how could it be possible to explain the way to reach it, Swamiji" she hesitated.

"Why not.. ...To say how to prepare tomato soup one need

not have tasted it before. He can very well say how to prepare it and likewise you can speak about the way to attain Self-knowledge."

The devotee was satisfied with swamiji's answer and started giving her short speech. After prayer Swamiji returned back to his Kutir.

8th JANUARY 1960

CONVERSION AND NOT COMPULSION

When writing a letter to a person against whom some complaints, that he is collecting money from devotees in the name of Swamiji, were received, Swamiji wrote the following to that person concerned:

"I AM RECEIVING COMPLAINTS AGAINST YOUR NOBLE SELF.
BE ON THE ALERT. ATTAIN THE
'ATMIC WEALTH'

Here we find the difference between an ordinary boss and a sagely Master. An ordinary man on hearing such complaints, immediately gets excited, takes all sorts of action, starts condemning the person and even publish in newspapers against him. But Swamiji, the sagely master knows and understands the capacity as well as the weakness of human beings who are in the process of becoming divine. Swamiji understands that every experience, we get, bitter or sweet, is only a stepping stone towards the goal eternal, is only a moulding unto the shape divine. Therefore whenever he finds such sort of weakness, such sort of inferior qualities in any man, Swamiji never condemns it, he never hates him, he never gets angry with him, but simply points out to him the correct way and gives him the positive advice.

"Attain the Atmic wealth" see the force in the sentence. It will directly penetrate the heart of the person concerned when he reads. ... . Instead of writing to the person by pointing directly his cheat in a negative way and irritating him, Swamiji gives a mild dose and converts him. He simply places the fact before him for him to reflect and realise himself. The fact is, "O man! you have lost your understanding power. You may get some money now in some way or other, but understand, as it came so

170

it will go. What remains is only your guilty consciousness. Attain, therefore, the Atmic wealth, the imperishable wealth which gives you eternal satisfaction. This is Swamiji's method of conversion by love and not compulsion by force.

HERE LIES THE DIFFICULTY

A devotee brought some savoury, some fried grams packed in a plastic bag and offered it to Swamiji.

"Will it produce Diarrhoea, Doctor?" Swamiji turned towards Sri Swami Hridayananda.

"No Swamiji, it won't.... if we take a littl.e

"My goodness .... there lies the difficulty...The problem is we cannot take a little" Swamiji remarked.

All laughed.

In one of his books Swamiji has written that if one takes food only to satisfy his hunger, there will be no food shortage in the world then. It is a fact, the practice of which, of course, is very difficult. Suppose there is a burning of fire, any kind of water will do to put it off...Ganges water, well water or any muddy water will do... Similarly the hunger also is like a burning fire. Any kind of food will do and even taste delicious when you feel hungry. The stomach won't say "I want this, I don't want that;" it is only the sentry at the gate to the inner chamber, the rude man who has his own whims and fancies, tastes and temperaments. The tongue is the sentry at the gate. He alone says, "I want only this, I don't want that, it is good and that is bad." That which the tongue likes, is not suitable for the stomach. That which is good for the stomach, the tongue never likes it and refuses to send inside. For example, sweets he welcomes, but it is bad for the stomach, bitter things he refuses but they are very good for the stomach. So Swamiji's remark 'there lies the difficulty' points out to us a fact, points out to us, our slavishness to the tongue which alone is the cause for all the disease of the body.

Swamiji gave Darshan this morning at 9-30 a.m. When Swamiji was about to start to the office a devotee came and prostrated before him.

"How are you, sir?" Swamiji kindly enquired of him.

He started narrating his worldly difficulties and finally finished saying, "Swamiji, now I am fish out of water."

"Then go into the water" Swamiji suggested him.

"That is why I have come here Swamiji. You are the ocean of mercy. Now I will become alright."

Yes, Swamiji is a vast ocean, not only of mercy as the devotee described, but also of knowledge and wisdom, so much so Swamiji is able to take in thousands of men and women who are scorched in the fire of Samsar, in his compassionate heart which knows neither shore nor limit.

SOUTH AFRICANS' RELATIVE

Then Swamiji proceeded to the office. After prayer and Kirtan, Swamiji was engaged in his usual routine work.

A few devotees from South Africa came and prostrated.

"Have you any relatives in India," Swamiji enquired of them.

"No, Swamiji. Our ancestors had settled in South Africa in the year 1886. We were born there and so we don't know any of our relatives here. Only Swamiji is the relative to us now."

"They have worked hard and you are enjoying now. Is it not so," Swamiji remarked.

The Divine Life Movement has spread in South Africa to such an extent, devotees from various parts of Africa come here to India just to have Darshan of Swamiji. Even though India is their Mother Land they have none to call their own, except Swa-

Even a short stay with Swamiji makes the South African devotees feel so homely, they have no inclination even to visit other parts of India, to see places of interest. The reason is, in their Mother Land they have Swamiji, the father, mother and Friend Divine, from whom they get solace and comfort to their heart's content.

POINTS TO REMEMBFR ALWAYS

Remember: without reverence and obedience to Guru or the preceptor and without his grace, the aspirant cannot have success in the practice of Yoga.

Remember: Egoism casts delusion on man. It causes forgetfulness of good thoughts and forces him to entertain evil thoughts and do evil action. Eradicate egoism to its very root.

Remember: without intense dispassion and burning aspiration, regularity in meditation, the aspirants cannot reach the goal.

Remember: dispassion and Sadhana (Vairagya and Abhyasa) are the two wings with which you can soar to the realm of eternal bliss.

Remember: if dispassion wanes, if Sadhana is slackened, if meditation becomes irregular, temptations are waiting to pull you down and throw you in the dark abyss.

Remember: if there are cheerfulness, joy, peace on the face, know that the seeker is progressing in meditation. If there are gloom and depression on the face, know that the aspirant is under the influence of Tamas (inertia).

Remember: Brahman alone is real; this world is unreal; the individual soul is identical with Brahman.

Remember: egoism and the senses are your real enemies. Slay them ruthlessly through self-surrender and self-restraint.

Remember: this world is impermanent, unreal and full of

pains, sorrows, diseases and death; and God is full of bliss, peace and wisdom.

FATHER IS GOD

An old man with a young boy came and prostrated before Swamiji.

"Is it your father" Swamiji enquired of the boy.

"Yes Swamiji."

"Serve your father well. Father is the visible god on earth. Obey him and worship him." Swamiji advised the boy.

The old man was very much pleased with Swamiji's advice to his son.

VISION OF PERFECTION

It was about 4 o'clock in the evening. A stout young man was carried and brought on a stretcher to the Sivananda General Hospital. The man on the stretcher was seriously wounded. Blood was oozing all over his face, and the face was swollen. Two policemen surrounded by a little crowd were coming along.

The Policemen were enquiring for the doctor. Dr. Prahlad and D. Punjabi came after a while and attended on the patient.

First-aid was given. His wounds were dressed. He was practically unconscious.

Then came forward the policeman with the story of the person.

He narrated....

"His name is Sri D.K. Roy. He is a decoit. He used to hide on the branches of the trees on the roadside waiting for the passersby. Man, woman, young or old, anyone who comes that way alone, he jumps on them, frightens and threatens them and robs away whatever they have, money or jewels, etc.

This is his regular occupation. It so happened, yesterday he did the same thing with a middle aged villager who was passing that way. The villager somehow escaped him and returned with 3 more persons to attack him. But this fellow, hiding on the branches, threw stones on these men and they ran away. They reported the matter to the police. Then both the villagers, and some policemen joined together and rounded him up. But somehow the decoit escaped and started running while the villagers and the police started chasing him from both the directions.

He couldn't escape and while running, unfortunately, fell in a wayside pit, about 20 feet deep, broke his six teeth and suffered severe wounds all over his body.

Then the villagers got down to the pit, took him and brought him out. By the time we reached the hospital here, he became unconscious."

The Policeman finished his story and the crowd of curiosity-mongers dispersed and went their way. Soon the news spread all over the place, and Dilip Kumar Roy became the showroom exhibit. Each one came, saw him, some took pity on him; some scolded him and said that he deserves the punishment, and made all sorts of gossips and remarks about wounded unconscious man.

It was now 8 o'clock. Swamiji emerged out from his Kutir and was proceeding towards the Satsang Bhavan. The news about the decoit was given to him. Swamiji heard calmly and was proceeding forward. On the way he entered the hospital ward, where the injured was lying. Swamiji came near him and stood for a while. Each one, gathered there was anxious to hear Swamiji's reaction and remarks. Swamiji calmly stood for a few minutes.

"Let us now chant Maha Mrityunjaya Mantra for the health and speedy recovery of Dilip Kumar Roy." So saying he started chanting 'Triyambakam.....

After the chanting was over, Swamiji called someone to bring a biscuit-tin from his Kutir. Biscuit-tin was brought. He kept it near him. 'Lord Narayana has come in this form. Please give him the biscuits, in the morning with tea or milk', so saying he calmly proceeded.

A serene silence prevailed there. Devotees were looking at Swamiji in a sort of reflecting mood.

"Is Swamiji, Jesus re-incarnated?"

Is Swamiji, the Buddha, re-appeared?" "Is Swamiji, the Tulsidas or Kabir?"

"Is He Guru Nanak or what else is he then?"

Such were the anxious inquiring looks of the devotees, both Western and Indian, who were coming along with Swamiji.

"Bol Satguru Maharaj Ki Jai."

This sound brought the devotees down once again from their reflecting moods. Then only did they realise that they had reached the Satsangh Hall.

Any commentary or interpretation on the above incident, if at all needed by any one, is, that Swamiji's vision is one of perfection which sees only the Reality, breaking through all the barriers of name and form, quality and character in all beings. The thief in our eyes is the Lord Narayana in his vision.

This is the vision of perfection, this is the vision of a Sage, this is Sivananda's vision!

This is not what I say, my friends, but what the Flute-bearer of Brindavan says:

Vidya-vinaya-sampanne brahmane gavi hastini
Shuni chaiva shwapake cha panditah samadarshinah

10th JANUARY 1960

ADVICE TO ASPIRANTS

After the night Satsang today, Sri Atmaram was asking someone the whereabouts of certain Swami who is touring all over India, collecting money from devotees for his American tour, the only ambition of his life. Swamiji hearing the conversaion made the following remark.

'Nowadays it has become a disease for the aspirants. They take Sannyas, learn some Upanishad and Gita, study some pages in psychology and science and fly to America for preaching. That is all their ambition in life. They think that they have achieved everything by doing so. They are not bothered to develop their inner personality, they are not bothered to gain the inner spiritual strength, they are not bothered to reform themselves in Spirit before reforming others. The result is, they lose even the little aspiration they possess in the beginning by moving too much in the society. Their words become empty bullets. Mere words will not have the capacity to transform a man unless they come from the heart. Therefore aspirants should kill this kind of Samskaras in the bud itself, otherwise the path they walk only lead to destruction and nowhere else."

11th JANUARY 1960

THE BEST BARBER

"Who is the best Barber, Atmaramji?" After the morning prayer was over in the office, Swamiji put this above question.

Atmaramji was expecting the reply from Swamiji himself.

"God is the best barber. . . .Because .... Barber shaves only the hair, but they again grow. God shaves the Vasanas (the impressions in the mind) but they grow not again. So He is the Supreme Barbar," and Swamiji added, "God alone has to shave our Vasanas .... only by God's Grace we can annihilate our Vasanas. . . .But for HIS Grace all our efforts become vain."

"What are the five ways to increase the longevity of life?" Next question started from Swamiji.

All were expecting the reply from Swamiji himself.

"First is the practice of Viparita Karani Mudra. Second is Jalandharabandha. Third is Practice of Kumbhak. Fourth is Brahmacharya and fifth is Trayambaka Mantra Japa.

VIPARITAKARANI MUDRA: Lie on the ground. Raise the legs up, straight. Support the buttocks with the hands. Rest elbows on the ground. Remain steady. This is Viparita Karani Mudra. Start this practice with minute duration and increase the period gradually to three hours. According to the Yoga Sastras, in the region of navel there lies the Yogic Centre called Manipura Chakra or Epigastric Plexus and in the region of throat lies the Vishuddha Chakra or Laryngeal Plexus or Pharyngeal Plexus, which is the origin of the Palate. Life energy or the nectar of moon in the Yogic terminology is oozing from Sahasrara drop by drop, through the palate and the fire in the navel, i.e., sun in the Yoga-Term absorbs this nectar and so man's life is decreased. But by the practice of Viparitakarani Mudra the position of the sun and the moon are reversed. So the Nectar of the moon instead of going downward takes the course up-ward. Therefore man's longevity of life is increased.

JALANDHARA BANDHA: Contract the throat. Press the chin firmly against the chest. This is Jalandhara Bandha. It should be practised at the end of Purak (inhalation) and at the beginning of Kumbhak (Retention). The gastric fire which is situated in the region of navel consumes the nectar which exudes out of the Sahasrara Chakra or thousand petalled lotus in the upper cere-bral region through the hole in the palate. This Bandha prevents the nectar thus being consumed. So man's Life is increased.

KUMBHAK: Man breaths 21000 times a day at the rate of 15 breaths a minute. By the practice of retention of breath or Kumbhak man saves the Pranic energy and thus his longevity of life is increased.

And all of you know about Brahmacharya and Trayamabakam Mantra. Besides this, Sattwic Diet and Yoga Asans are also helpful.

"Worrylessness also makes a man live long. Is it not Swamiji?" Someone asked.

"Of course. ....but is there any man who is not worrying for something or other in this world." Swamiji replied.

"But Swamiji is there who is not worrying for anything", Sri Swami Lalithanandaji remarked. All appreciated and ap-proved of her answer.

"For me!....No worry you say! .... I am the most worrying man in this world. As soon as I get up in the morning, my first worry is whether the carpenter whom Sri Lalithanandaji asked for some work in her room, has gone there or not" When Swamiji was telling this the whole office room was burst into laughter.

"Sri Atmaramji, tell me, what is concentration, what is meditation and what is Samadhi?"

Sri Atmaramji gave some round-about answer. Then Swamiji himself cleared it.

"Concentration is fixing the mind on a particular object, or form but when you concentrate, there appear the thoughts of so many things. They appear in the marginal consciousness. But meditation is a continuous flow of thought on a particular object or form or idea. When the Dhyata and Dhyeya (meditator and the object of meditation) both become one and meditation drops. This state is Samadhi."

TWENTY IMPORTANT SPIRITUAL INSTRUCTIONS

1. Get up at 4 a.m. daily. This is Brahmamuhurta which is extremely favourable for meditation on God.

2. **Asana:** Sit on Padma, Siddha or Sukha Asana for Japa and meditation for half an hour, facing the East or the North. Increase the period gradually to three hours. Do Sirshasana and Sarvangasana for keeping up Brahmacharya and health. Take light physical exercises such as walking, etc., regularly. Do twenty Pranayamas.

3. **Japa:** Repeat any Mantra as pure Om or Om Namo Narayanaya, Om Namah Sivaya, Om Namo Bhagavate Vasudevaya, Om Sri Saravanabhavaya Namah, Sita Ram, Sri Ram, Hari Om, or Gayatri, according to your taste or inclination, from 108 to 21,600 times daily.

4. **Dietetic Discipline:** Take Sattvic food, Suddha Ahara. Give up chillies, tamarind, garlic, onion, sour articles, oil, mustard, asafoetida. Observe moderation in diet (Mitahara). Do not overload the stomach. Give up those things which the mind likes best for a fortnight in a year. Eat simple food. Milk and fruits help concentration. Take food as medicine to keep the life going. Eating for enjoyment is sin. Give up salt and sugar for a month. You must be able to live on rice, Dhal and bread without any chutney. Do not ask for extra salt for Dhal and sugar for tea, coffee or milk.

5. Have a separate meditation-room under lock and key.

6. **Charity:** Do charity regularly, every month, or even daily according to your means, say six paisa per rupee.

7. **Svadhyaya:** Study systematically the Gita, the Ramayana, the Bhagavata, Vishnu-Sahasranama, Lalita-Sahasranama, Aditya Hridaya, the Upanishads or the Yoga

Vasishtha, the Bible, the Zend Avesta, the Koran, the Tripitakas, the Granth Sahib, etc., from half an hour to one hour daily, and have Suddha Vichara.

8. **Brahmacharya:** Preserve the vital force (Veerya) very, very carefully. Veerya is God in motion or manifestation—Vibhuti. Veerya is all power. Veerya is all money. Veerya is the essence of life, thought and intelligence.

9. **Prayer Slokas:** Get by heart some prayer Slokas, Stotras and repeat them as soon as you sit in the Asana before starting Japa or meditation. This will elevate the mind quickly.

10. **Satsanga:** Have Satsanga. Give up bad company, smoking, meat and alcoholic liquors entirely. Do not develop any evil habits.

11. **Fast on Ekadasi:** Fast on Ekadasi or live on milk and fruits only.

12. **Japa Mala:** Have a Japa Mala (rosary) round your neck or in your pocket or underneath your pillow at night.

13. **Mouna:** Observe Mouna (vow of silence) for a couple of hours daily.

14. **Speak the Truth:** Speak the truth at all costs. Speak a little. Speak sweetly.

15. **Reduce your wants:** Reduce your wants. If you have four shirts, reduce the number to three or two. Lead a happy, contented life. Avoid unnecessary worry. Have plain living and high thinking.

16. **Never hurt anybody:** Never hurt anybody *(ahimsa paramo dharmah)*. Control anger by love, Kshama (forgiveness) and Daya (compassion).

17. **Do not depend upon servants:** Do not depend upon servants. Self-reliance is the highest of all virtues.

18. **Self-analysis:** Think of the mistakes you have com-

mitted during the course of the day, just before retiring to bed (self-analysis). Keep daily diary and self-correction register. Do not brood over past mistakes.

19. **Fulfil duties:** Remember that death is awaiting you at every moment. Never fail to fulfil your duties. Have pure conduct (Sadachara).

20. **Surrender to God:** Think of God as soon as you wake up and just before you go to sleep. Surrender yourself completely to God (Saranagati).

This is the essence of all spiritual Sadhanas.
This will lead you to Moksha.
All these Niyamas or spiritual canons must be rigidly observed.
You must not give leniency to the mind.

—Swami Sivananda